LIFE
MAKEOVER

LIFE MAKEOVER

EMBRACE THE BOLD, BEAUTIFUL, AND BLESSED YOU

DOMINIQUE SACHSE

NELSON
BOOKS

An Imprint of Thomas Nelson

ISBN 978-1-4002-2572-9 (HC)
ISBN 978-1-4002-2573-6 (eBook)

Library of Congress Cataloging-in-Publication Data

Names: Sachse, Dominique, 1967- author.
Title: Life makeover / Dominique Sachse.
Description: Nashville : Thomas Nelson, 2022. | Summary: "Three-time Emmy Award-winning newscaster and popular YouTube and social media encourager, Dominique Sachse delivers a powerful call to women to embrace their outward beauty as the first step in living with internal boldness, confidence, and renewed joy"-- Provided by publisher.
Identifiers: LCCN 2021045168 (print) | LCCN 2021045169 (ebook) | ISBN 9781400225729 (hardcover) | ISBN 9781400225736 (ebook)
Subjects: LCSH: Women--Religious life. | Feminine beauty (Aesthetics) | Beauty, Personal.
Classification: LCC BV4527 .S2195 2022 (print) | LCC BV4527 (ebook) | DDC 248.8/43--dc23
LC record available at https://lccn.loc.gov/2021045168
LC ebook record available at https://lccn.loc.gov/2021045169

Printed in the United States of America

22 23 24 25 26 LSC 10 9 8 7 6 5 4 3 2

To you, the reader, for whom this book is written and to me, the author, for whom these words are needed.

CONTENTS

A NOTE TO THE READER

THIS BOOK IS FOR EVERY woman who has ever found herself adrift in unknown waters, as if she woke up one day living a life wholly unfamiliar to her and seemingly powerless to chart a new course.

It is equally for every woman who has felt as if she's lost in a sea of other people's needs or drowning in endless responsibilities.

And it is for every woman who has been simply swept away, her identity all but forgotten in the tidal wave of life.

If you recognize yourself in any of these scenarios, as I do, take heart. I have made it my mission to throw you a life preserver and teach you how to navigate your way back to yourself. Together we will set our feet firmly on solid ground so that we have the freedom to take deep, refreshing breaths and to live our lives as we truly desire. And from there we will embark on a bold journey fueled by faith, purpose, and intention.

INTRODUCTION

· ·

A BRIDGE TO YOU

I SAT THERE IN MY BATHROOM, fiddling with my phone in front of the mirror. *There.* I had just the right angle, left arm extended and right arm ready to do the work. Not completely sure how to begin, I just smiled into my iPhone and said, "Hi, there! Dominique here. I have been getting so many questions from you, my TV viewers, about . . . well, my eye makeup of all things. I've answered dozens of you by email, but I thought it might be simpler and more effective to show you. So, here it goes."

I proceeded to demonstrate just how to achieve my signature "smoky eye" look. The muscles in my left arm started burning like fire as I tried to hold the cell phone steady while my right arm whisked, blended, and smudged. I offered encouraging words like, "Don't worry if it ends up looking more like a black eye than a smoky eye, because you can just wipe it off and try again. Have fun with it." And then I ended by saying, "Keep on sending me questions; I love hearing from you." I posted the video on my "official" Facebook page, the one I had through the

Houston station where I anchored the evening news, wondering aloud if it was really such a good idea.

The response was almost instantaneous, and comments started pouring in.

> *Ding.* "Thank you, Dominique! I am going to try this tonight!"
> *Ding.* "You make it seem so easy. I can't wait to do it. What's your favorite eye shadow?"
> *Ding.* "This is so cool! Thank you for sharing! Now talk to me about your hair."

And on it went. There were *thousands* of them. And I was floored. I had often joked that it didn't matter what I said on the air because the vast majority of viewer comments focused on my hairstyle, makeup, or wardrobe. I could report, "The earth has just imploded," and someone would write in saying, "I'm not so sure about that blouse on you."

Luckily, I have a sense of humor. And I've known for a long time that we're judged first on our appearance; intellect, character, and personality come later. So maybe I shouldn't have been so surprised by the overwhelming response to my smoky-eye tutorial. But one thing I knew for sure: this was the start of something new, and my smoky eyes were wide open as to where it would all lead.

Eight years, one YouTube channel, and nearly two million subscribers later, I have been privileged to witness more women grab hold of my content and use it to transform their lives than I could ever have fathomed. There is no question in my mind that God ordered my steps on this pathway, and I am grateful for it every single day.

What did all those viewers asking about my appearance teach me?

Image matters.

Whether it's fair or not, we can't change the fact that the way we look is powerful. It's the thing that gets our foot in the door, wherever that door may lead. So rather than ignoring that fact or trying to change it, let's lean into that notion and use it to generate change within us. Let's consider *beauty from the outside in.*

That's where we're going to start in this book—by flipping the script on beauty. True beauty may ultimately come from within, and it *is* important to develop that inner beauty. But I've found it really helpful to start on the outside and work my way in. In fact, what we do on the outside directly influences what happens on the inside.

Here's what I mean. Read any self-help book and you'll find that improving your happiness, increasing your level of fulfillment, or reconnecting with your passions and purpose—those are *processes.* They don't happen overnight, so they require patience. You can't rush the development of inner beauty. But the good news is: you *can* rush your appearance. And working on your appearance can give you a jump start on developing the rest of you.

It doesn't matter if you've had the same hairstyle for decades, if your makeup bag is collecting dust, or if you don't wear 90 percent of the clothes in your closet. I'm going to give you some of my tried-and-true tips and tricks to get you looking and feeling fantastic while you're on the road to becoming truly beautiful. I'll show you how to "fake it till you make it." Because when you invest time and energy into your appearance, you'll begin to feel better about all the rest of your life too. I believe by working on the outside first, you will become motivated to live each day as the very best version of yourself because you'll be so intrigued by what you're seeing in the mirror.

Even so, this is not a "beauty" book. It's a book about getting where you want to be in your life, about becoming the best version of you there is. But the beauty-from-the-outside-in approach can work like a pistol shot at a track meet that propels you off the blocks. Making a physical change acts as a kick start for the deeper work that follows.

If you're thinking, *I'll flame out*—trust me, you won't. You'll be so excited about the new you that is emerging that you won't want to stop. Seeing yourself differently will motivate you to start doing your life differently. The self-esteem you begin to build may start on the outside, but it will lead you to take a deeper dive into examining your whole life.

I have heard from thousands of women about a specific moment when they caught an unexpected glimpse of themselves in the mirror. The words they use to describe that moment are almost exactly the same: "I don't even know that person. She looks so tired and ragged." They, like so many women I know, have been so overwhelmed with all that is going on in their lives that they have lost touch with their true selves—both inside and outside.

I want you to pause and inhale this thought deeply: *you deserve more, and you can have it.* The whole purpose of this book is to show you how. I'm going to give you surprisingly simple tools for your transformation, your life makeover, equipping you to take back the power in your life and begin making changes today.

I'd like you to think of this book as a bridge you're building to yourself. Every day another piece of material is laid to move you forward. And every day your confidence grows and you take another step across. As you move through the chapters in this book, your bridge will become stronger, and you'll soon tango across it with maneuvers that look effortless on the outside but are stoked with boldness on the inside.

In order for you to take this journey, though, I need you to say and believe one essential truth about yourself: *I am my most valuable investment.*

Believing this may be counterintuitive. In fact, it may go against everything you currently think or have heard. You may be held back by thoughts like, *I can't be selfish.* Or you may be facing some time-consuming realities, such as raising children, taking care of aging parents, or tackling a demanding job, and after a day of one (or more) of those, you're just happy to crawl into bed.

Here's the thing, though. You won't be as good as you could be in any of those roles unless you start prioritizing yourself. Believing that you have something to contribute—that you are worthy of the investment of time, effort, attention, and love— puts out a message: "Get ready. I'm about to *do* something special, *be* someone special, and help myself and others *feel* special."

If you believe with all your heart, mind, and soul that you are your most valuable investment, that belief will serve as the foundation for your journey. It's what will give you the confidence to step forward, knowing that your better self—and ultimately your better life—is out there. And you'll be ready to take the bold moves necessary to get it. You'll learn to *be bold and be blessed.*

Does it seem strange to think of yourself as bold? You can be! In fact, to get where you want to get in life, you need to be. Bold means being willing to take a risk, and risk-taking is essential for finding the kind of life you dream of. I'll encourage you to make bold moves, and I'll start by sharing personal examples of times when I took risks and reaped rewards. I'll also share a few of my failures—and how I learned and grew by allowing myself to be vulnerable to those failures. And I will lay out some practical suggestions for being bold, good starting points to get your mind flowing.

The great thing about being bold is that it can be applied to every area of your life. If you're willing to take the risk, you can pave the way to a satisfying and rewarding marriage, career, lasting friendships, and more. Bold moves are contagious and limitless. Being bold is an action, not a reaction. It puts you in the driver's seat.

But here's something that is often overlooked in our high-pressure society: to be bold, we also must discover *the unexpected power of rest*. Rest's role is paramount to living bold and blessed. It gives us the energy to take those important risks.

I know you're tired. How can you not be? Women tend to take on so much and take so little care of themselves. But rest is crucial. Research has proven how powerful it is. Our new fitness gadgets have even begun to measure rest and sleep because companies have learned what a difference it makes.

I'm going to share with you some different forms of rest because when you're overworked, overstressed, and under rested, you don't do anything well. In building a bridge to a better you, a loose screw or an improperly tightened joint can cause the bridge to collapse. Take your time and get the rest you need to stay sharp and focused. Yawning from exhaustion is so yesterday!

Overcoming fears goes hand in hand with embracing bold

risk. Both are important because you can't have one without letting go of the other. Fear is the biggest enemy blocking our bridge building. Fear of falling, fear of failing. Fear is crippling and leaves you standing in place questioning whether you should even be there at all, not to mention moving forward. It causes catastrophic physiological changes in our bodies, reduces oxygen flow, raises cortisol levels, and locks our minds into a limiting mentality.

There are many strategies for overcoming fear. I want to encourage you to fight fear with faith. I'll touch on my faith journey, which initially started with having faith in myself but led to an exploration of my faith in God. You may be surprised to learn that this was a later-in-life epiphany for me. But I've learned that God meets us right where we are, willingly and joyfully. There are blessings to be counted each day, no matter how little you think you have to be grateful for. I want you to look for those blessings, thank God for them, pray big, bold prayers for seeking more in your life, and press into your faith when challenges arise. I also want you to learn when it's appropriate to move on. You'll find yourself living with more courage than you ever thought you had.

Creativity and hobbies are integral parts of this journey because they allow for our whole selves to shine and for that bridge to sparkle. If you feel your life is all work and no play, then my belief that hobbies are not just fun, but essential, will appeal to you.

You might be thinking, *I barely have time for a nap, let alone an art class.* But could it be you've lost your connection with that child inside you—the little girl who took sidewalk chalk and turned ordinary concrete into her own canvas, the young artist who blended her paint perfectly to capture a warm sunset on the horizon, the tomboy who rode her surfboard and dodged crashing waves, or the showstopping dancer who pivoted and sauntered in glittery delight across a wooden floor? Those early pursuits lit a fire within you back then. They gave you pleasure, sparked your creativity, supplied purpose and measurable growth. It's time to get in touch with that little girl once more. That's why *it's time to get a hobby.*

Just writing these descriptions was like casting a reel back into my own childhood, conjuring up images and emotion with every keystroke. The eight-year-old version of us was encouraged in this pursuit. Yet once we stop skipping, singing, swaying, or making, we somehow feel it's just not important anymore.

My own trips back to childhood hobbies or the creation of new ones reminded me why they're just as necessary today as they were yesterday. And what's even better about today is that you may discover you have a new talent, interest, or ability that wasn't there before. I want you to harness that new joy and feel creativity brewing again. You can paint that bridge of yours a shiny gold or go more natural and subtle, get creative with stone placement, iron, or steel. How exciting to imagine the options!

This leads to what I think is the obvious: it's crucial that we never stop learning. And one of the best ways to involve ourselves in ongoing learning is to discover *the magic of mentoring.*

Sometimes we just have to stop and ask for help and advice. We don't know everything, and we certainly aren't expected to. I've sought help from trustworthy sources and asked pertinent questions along the way when the answers didn't appear on their own. I hope you will look for opportunities to do this while you're engaged in bridge construction. But I also hope you'll look for the chance to *be* a mentor. Someone you know might be on the same journey you are and could certainly benefit from your experience. The more notches we have on our life belt, the more we should cinch this opportunity. The gift is in the giving, and you never know how far-reaching your wisdom or care will go in someone else's life.

In order to learn something new, we have to be taught. But we also learn by being the teacher. Whether in the role of teacher or student (both of which can happen at any age), we all have the opportunity to impart wisdom or to absorb it.

Finally, a bold, beautiful, and blessed you is a picture of class, a woman who is graceful and confident, poised and knowledgeable. It's the inside and outside of you, symbiotically paired and balanced and on full display.

Classy means stylish and sophisticated. Your bridge will not only be seen by you but all those around you. What feeling do you want it to convey? How would you want to describe it?

Class involves both looks and behavior, appearing and being. It's easy to identify a classy woman when you see her. She enters the room with her head high and shoulders back, confident and assured. She's not aloof. In fact, she's quite aware of her surroundings, catching an eye with a warm smile in return. She gives the impression of dignity and poise. She dresses with taste, clothing her shape with cognizance of both her frame and frame of mind. She speaks from a place of knowledge and listens with respect to opinion, never hastily offering her own. She's a fine wine, a painting, a poem to be observed, appreciated, and enjoyed.

Some would say that class is becoming a lost art, but I believe it's one worth cultivating. If that woman I described above speaks to you, then you might find my thoughts on keeping it classy helpful. I'll guide you through the beautiful, elegant, and simple ways to bring an air of class to everything you do. Who doesn't want to complete their bridge with style points?

So here we are, standing on one side of the expanse staring at the other. We need to build a bridge to connect to this new land; otherwise, we can't move forward and will miss the detailed view below. But the pathway there means acquiring the tools necessary to build that bridge.

Each woman's bridge will be as unique as she is. One piece of steel, wood, and concrete at a time, enabling her horizontal journey. Several vertical pillars will be needed to support it. The building process is a joyful one; each day it will connect you to something meaningful about yourself.

I am here for you throughout. This book is my bridge to you. Take that first step. I promise the terrain below isn't foreign. It is the soil, water, vegetation, and life that is *you*.

Take a good look. Is it healthy, green, and well-tended, or do you feel it's a little too arid and lacking the beauty and sustainability you desire? If so, I want to share my tools for the proper placement and care of your outer and inner life so that what you see is lush and nurtured from your high vantage point. Beauty below and beauty in the discovery of the unknown.

I want to equip you with the tools I've used to reach new lands—tools that will enliven your soul, free you from the fear of looking down, and sharpen your vision as you move forward.

This is your bridge—the bridge to your best future. Let's start building it.

ONE

· ·

BEAUTY FROM THE
OUTSIDE IN

BEAUTY. SO SUBJECTIVE YET SO powerful. We seek it in the world around us and within ourselves. We covet it. Try to create it. Fear losing it. And we understand the power of it.

Case in point: Have you ever been faced with a presentation in front of the boss at work—or a job interview, a first date, or family gathering—about which you were stressed or unsure? And have you ever looked in the mirror beforehand and added a bold red lipstick or a little extra mascara to help you gain that self-confidence? It's quite amazing how well-applied makeup or a new hairstyle can boost your confidence and put you in a new frame of mind.

Professional makeup artist Bobbi Brown has said that "all women are pretty without makeup and can be pretty powerful with even just a touch of makeup."[1] When I started receiving all those comments after I posted my smoky-eye tutorial, I realized just how true that statement is. When you take a step back and look in the mirror after mastering a new makeup technique, you feel as if you can take on the world. It's really quite magical.

As I began to connect with more women online and see just how much confidence I was able to instill in them through makeup, I started to peel back the layers a bit to see what was really underneath. And the community did not disappoint in their willingness to be open, honest, and transparent, to share their own stories, fears, failures, and triumphs. As a result, my message has evolved and continues to do so. Sprinkled in my beauty and lifestyle tutorials that started in 2014 are little messages about cultivating what lies within, where true beauty and joy originate. No amount of makeup illuminates like the glow that comes from a self-actualized, satisfied woman. Hair and makeup techniques are just the icing on the cake.

The Moment in the Mirror

I have been so fortunate to receive letters from women around the world describing a particular moment when a certain video of mine, or even a series of videos, resonated with where they were in life. That was when they grabbed the bull by the horns and started making the changes they felt were necessary.

One woman described how she went from not caring for or about herself and being quite depressed to suddenly feeling motivated to start with the basics in makeup and investigate new hairstyles and skin care products. Feeling excited about the changes she was seeing, she figured, *why stop*? She tweaked her diet and kept working on herself both internally and externally.

She expressed how important the exterior was to kick-start the harder, deeper work inside. Toward the end of her incredibly open and heartfelt letter, she shared how reinvigorated she felt. She had gone from not caring at all to examining all her options with optimism and curiosity. And it all started with watching a video and deciding to make just one little change.

I really believe such defining moments are a test. God knows that if we see it through, He'll bring us out better in the end. This lovely woman dug in her heels and learned resiliency. She also clearly stated what I will discuss in this chapter, and that is the effectiveness of *beauty from the outside in*.

The truth is, there's a lot of value in adopting a "fake it till you make it" mentality. You may be yearning to make over your entire life, which is a process, but what is the one thing you can do right now? Where can you start for immediate results? A new hairstyle, makeup look, wardrobe change, or all of the above?

I embarked on my exploration of all things beauty and transformation when I was young, and I will share some enlightening experiences—and at times quite humorous examples—throughout this book. Hopefully you'll be able to relate or not feel so bad about your own experimentation. As they say, "No risk it, no biscuit!"

First Appearances

When I started my TV news career and I was transitioning from being a traffic reporter to news anchor, I had to learn on the job. Quickly. Every morning was a new opportunity to hone my overall look, presentation, and skill set, and not every newscast was a win. While I was working away on developing my craft as a journalist, I was also trying to define my image.

Big jewelry and scarves were all the rage back then, but I can tell you firsthand that trying to keep a scarf still—rather than sticking up in all different directions and becoming a total distraction for the duration of a newscast—is impossible. I had to learn not to succumb to certain trends.

As I was working toward creating my own signature style—one that stood out above the stereotypical, cookie-cutter news anchor look—I vividly recall a newscast when I took a risk with my hair. It was the early 1990s, and "big hair" was still the popular look of the day. That day I opted to lower my hair and pull it back away from my face—not in a ponytail, just up and off my jawline and falling behind my shoulders. I don't know what possessed me, really, but rather than my usual "poof" of long, reddish-brown, wavy hair, I chose this new look. It was a decisive change, and I had no idea how it would look on camera.

To my surprise, I received many compliments that day. People loved the change and commented that it was clean and classy. So I went back and watched a recorded copy of that newscast, and I could really see why it resonated. My new hairstyle looked sleeker and more controlled and helped give my overall presentation just the right note of professionalism, warmth, and precision.

I used that experience as a starting point for cultivating and enhancing my image as a news anchor. Not long afterward I took about six inches off my mane and brought it up to my shoulders. From there I went to a tight crop, almost like what broadcast journalist Jane Pauley liked to wear during her tenure on *The Today Show* from 1976 to 1989. This set the stage for what was soon to become my "signature" on air, which was to embrace and celebrate change, but always with certain truths underpinning the equation: class and sophistication. My hair color may have varied, my lengths may have shortened or lengthened somewhat, my makeup and clothing styles may have evolved, but my goal was always to convey the right overall picture.

My journey to become my best self didn't stop with my external appearance, of course. I've always understood the importance of first impressions, but I wanted my internal skill set not only to match what was seen but to elevate it. As I was making changes to my appearance and receiving feedback from viewers, I was also learning the ins and outs of broadcast journalism and how to become a better writer and broadcaster. I had to continue to dig, stretch, and challenge myself to be creative in every way. As my look evolved, so did my ability to communicate naturally and effectively. The whole woman was developing while I learned and lived the practical power of beauty from the outside in.

Not Necessarily a Disaster

I discovered at an early age that making a physical change is the quickest way to truly see ourselves differently. The first big decision I made early on was to my hair—at age twelve! My initiation to beauty from the outside in wasn't a total win, but it led to a cascading series of joyful experiments and outside-the-box bold moments that I still relish to this day.

It was a blisteringly hot Texas day in the summer of 1979. As we did almost every weekend, my mom and I headed down to Galveston, an island city southeast of Houston—just fifty minutes from my door to the Gulf of Mexico. Not known for its powdery sand or blue water, Galveston still offered expansive brownish beaches, water parks, cute boys, and icy treats, so I was all in. My mom loved to tan, Hawaiian Tropic tanning oil and all, so she supported my beachy interests.

That day I'd invited a friend, and we packed our usual sandwiches, drinks, and tanning potions. Something else made its way into the tote as well—two bottles of Sun In, a spray-on, heat-activated hair bleach. A mix of hydrogen peroxide, lemon juice, and other multisyllable names I wouldn't dare try to pronounce, that product was immensely popular with girls my age in the 1970s and '80s. You would spray it into your hair, let the heat of the sun work its magic, and presto—sun-streaked hair. Or at least that's what the bottle promised. The blonde teenager pictured on the label had the perfect placement of highlights around her all-American face, with a warm golden tan to offset the light hair and a neon-white smile just reeling me in.

Dark brown curly hair and all, I was determined to get the look. So once my mother and I were stretched out on our bright, colorful towels with mineral oil on our bodies and a touch of iodine to enhance our tans—I gasp now at the thought!—I took it upon myself to speed up the hair-lightening process. I took the spray nozzles off the bottles and poured the full contents of both on top of my head. Liquid cascaded down my long, brown tresses, each strand soaking in the chemical mixture.

Hours passed as we enjoyed the salt water and sand. My heart leaped in anticipation and delight, convinced that I would soon look just like the girl on the bottle.

As we drove home, my friend sat beside my mom in the front seat while I sat in the back. The air conditioner on full blast cooled down my burnt brown skin, still tingling from the Gulf's salty waters and the sun's rays, and also helped to dry my hair. I glanced up into our rearview mirror, hoping to see the great results I expected. A pit began to form in my stomach, and I could see my mom's eyes darting from the road to my face in that skinny rectangular mirror. We were watching my hair change color—not to the sunny tones pictured on the infamous box, but to a bright *orange!*

When we arrived home, I rushed inside and immediately ran to the shower. Shampoo, shampoo, condition, towel dry, wrap in a towel, wipe the steam off the mirror. My face was beet red from too much sun, and the roots of the front of my hair peeking out of the white towel wrapped around my head were still a light orange! I looked like a clown.

I unwrapped my newly colored hair and began to blow it dry section by section, tears rolling down my face. When I finished, I stormed out of the bathroom, immediately seeking my mom's comfort and her possible solution to this fiasco. As she caught full sight of me, in true Audrey fashion, she exclaimed, "I love it!" (I always joke that my mom is my agent. I can do no wrong in her eyes, and this moment clearly proved it.)

"How on earth could you love this hideous orange hair?" I inquired.

She immediately retorted, "It brightens up your face."

Ugh.

I went back to the pharmacy where I had purchased the Sun In and immediately started searching for a solution. When I asked advice from the ladies who worked behind the counter, they gasped and drawled, "Darlin', if you do anything else to your hayer, it's gawna fall out!"

Nail in the coffin.

I would have to ride this thing out.

As months crept by, I had the "rooty" look long before it was in. I dealt with middle school whispers, sneers, and jabs, and I had to look for other assets to play up while I was waiting for my new look to grow out—another great (but painful) lesson in not tying self-esteem to just one attribute. I was growing up as well as growing out, learning more about myself and those around me.

What Do You Have to Lose?

One of my favorite segments on *Today with Hoda and Jenna* is the Ambush Makeover with Louis Licari and Jill Martin. On those segments, a hopeful and unsuspecting woman in her prime is plucked from the audience, profiled as not having focused on her looks in a very long time, taken behind the scenes for a few hours in what could only be a beauty wonderland, and then revealed in the most public forum possible—in front of millions on TV.

Sight unseen, she's told to peek at herself in the mirror for the first time. Gasp! Hands to the face. Squeals from family as they lower their blindfolds. A tear might be shed on this newly made-over face—but only one tear, so as not to ruin the beautifully applied makeup. She twirls and pivots in delight, touching her hair and face and toying with her new outfit, not believing what the reflection holds. The audience at home is cheering her on and marveling at the transformation.

Then comes that lingering thought for those of us sitting on the couch and watching the show: *Should I do this to myself? Well, wait a minute—she had the best of the best making her over! How could she not look that marvelous surrounded by a team of skilled professionals making all the decisions for her? I could sit back and let that happen!*

And couldn't we all? A professional makeover would definitely take some of the hard work out of trying a new look. We've all seen the before and after in segments like that. Who wouldn't be there in the crowd with their hand-painted sign, hoping to be chosen?

But being made over on national TV is a needle-in-a-haystack scenario. For the rest of us, the thought process is more like, *I'm tired of looking this way. I want a change, but it's been so long, I don't know how to pull the trigger. How do I know what will look good on my face? What will work with my hair type? Then there's color. Do I want to make that kind of commitment? What if I hate it?*

So glad you asked! When you take a risk on a new look, you have a fifty-fifty chance of succeeding—but also of failing. Let's say you have an epic fail. Say you've gone in for a new haircut and color and you don't like the new look one bit.

I'm not even going to factor in what others think because I want you to get out of the habit of allowing that to dominate your decision-making. I'll have a lot to say on that a little later, but for now let's just say that *you* don't like it. Maybe you absolutely hate it. What's the worst that can happen?

You may be able to go back and tweak something. Or maybe not. Then you'll have to look at yourself in the mirror for a few weeks and not like the reflection. You may just have to endure an awkward growing-out process. None of that is fun, but it's not so awful when you think of it.

Is there an upside? Well, you may learn something about yourself. Maybe you'll actually learn to *like* the new look. But at the very least, you could learn that *you* are not a hairstyle, that your self-worth shouldn't be based on what's happening on your head. At the very least, you will have learned what it feels like to take a risk, to experience the downside. Well, check that one off the list. You knew it was possible. It happened. And guess what—you lived through it. Next time could bring the reward.

And wait a minute. Did you ever stop to think that in the growing-out process, in the tweaking and adjusting, you might find the best look for you—something you might never have known had you not gone there in the first place? You might discover a new styling skill set because you *had* to learn in the process. And a few months later—*bam!* Reward. These rewards far outweigh the initial fail. You pursued, persevered, and endured. You grew and developed skill. You looked for other attributes to play up during this season.

You leaped. You learned.

I'm feeling an Alanis Morissette song right about now.

New Hair, New You

I recently googled the definition of *expert*. Multiple sites define it as "a person with extensive knowledge or ability based on research, experience, or occupation and in a particular area of study."[2] I believe the transformations I've undertaken since my first experience with Sun In probably make me an expert in this particular area. My locks have been every color in the book, and my stylists know when they're blow-drying my hair to let me finish the do. They give me the brush and hair dryer and then shake their heads, sometimes appeasing me with, "She does it better than me."

They may or may not be right. Maybe they've just learned that this is the easiest way to cope with my control issues. But I do think my long experience in this area qualifies me as a bit of an expert.

Some of my favorite tutorials to create on YouTube involve styling hair: "4 Easy Short Hairstyles That Will Make You Want a Bob!," "How to Blow Out Side Swept Bangs," "Short Bob Blow Out for Sleek Volume!" My feeling is, if you're going to take the leap, I want to be a resource for you on how to style and care for your new hair. I want to show you that you're not stuck with just one look when you change your style.

So given this particular area of my expertise, I suggest starting your beauty-from-the-outside-in adventure with a fabulous new hairstyle.

Step #1: Create Your Vision

If you've followed me on YouTube for a while, you've seen me go from a pixie cut to long with hair extensions. You've seen me go from red to brown to blonde to chestnut to honey and on and on and on. One thing I can promise: I will never stay the same. I've learned to embrace this part of me, the chameleon who changes her cuts and colors based on what rock she chooses to inhabit.

So, now it's your turn. Time to create your own vision of where you want to go on this journey. Get your mind's eye wandering and exploring this great unknown. Don't set any limits at this point. Release the reins.

Maybe a variety of styles or colors appeal to you. Maybe

your dream is not all that far off from where you are now. Or maybe what you have in mind is a complete departure from what you've always done. Don't try to get too specific yet. Just keep looking and dreaming.

And where do you look? Hello, Pinterest! The catalog of ideas. Short hairstyles, blonde pixie, brown lob, auburn waves— they're all there for you to search. All shades, shapes, textures, lengths, ages, and stages.

I have to be honest: I have logged some serious hours on this site. Where do you think I get my inspo? That's right, the site with a red capital *P*. I think I have as many hairstyle screen grabs on my phone as I have pictures of my son, Styles. Okay, maybe not that many, but it's close.

The takeaway here is that you have a better chance of success with a new hairstyle if you spend some time researching exactly what you want—and have pictures to show the stylist. Collect images that reflect the new you, the woman you want to become. Pinterest is not the only possibility, of course. Many YouTube channels are dedicated to hair transformations. I, of course, like to provide a few on mine! If you see something you like, take a picture or a screen shot.

I do just that whenever I go in for a cut or color. Often I'll even text the photos the day before so the stylist will have time to mentally prepare for where we're going and maybe adjust the schedule if necessary. (Who knows? It might be necessary to block off an extra hour.)

The point of bringing pictures, as I tell my viewers on YouTube, is to not let ideas get lost in translation. You might think you're being absolutely clear: "So I want a bob, slightly angled from the back, textured but not too layered, a little wispy at the ends, above the shoulders but not at the jawline. Short but not too short, you know?" But your stylist's interpretation of those words can vary wildly from yours. The best way to prevent that from happening is to *show* your stylist what you're looking for. Present options not only for cut but for color. That could be another series of photos or even a video.

I've even been known to stop someone in a grocery store or restaurant when I see a hairstyle I love. I'll then ask to take their picture. Maybe you need to see your ideas in the living and moving flesh. What a compliment to the woman whose photo is being taken! And you'll get to capture all sides. It's also a great opportunity to ask, "Who did that?" Now you have a referral to a stylist who created a look you love—the next important step to a successful hair transformation.

Step #2: Find a Stylist—and Listen!

If I were to count the number of emails and direct messages from viewers who've asked, "Who does your hair?" or "Who did your hair when it looked like _____?" it would be a big number. These women are smart. They see something that resonates with them, and they want to go to the source. You can do that too. When you see a style you like, whether it's on a passerby or a local anchor, reach out to her and find out who and where.

Personal recommendations are invaluable in finding the right stylist, but an online search can be helpful as well. Search for top-rated salons in your area and read the reviews. And be sure to check out social media. Many salons and stylists have Instagram accounts for you to follow. It's the best way for them to promote their latest work and the best way for you to possibly see something or someone you like.

Once you locate a talented stylist you think you can trust, it's time to make an appointment and take the leap. Bring in your collected photos and hand them over. But don't be surprised if you hear, "I don't think this will work on you."

Screech! Needle off the record.

I can't tell you how many times this has happened to me. As a naturally dark, mousy-brown, curly-haired gal, I am drawn to lighter, straighter looks. It's always been that way. We are drawn to what we don't have. Got curls? You want poker-straight hair that can air dry to perfection. Got straight hair? You'd give anything for curl and wave and volume at the root. You struggle every time you style, only to have humidity bring down your do in a nanosecond. Cue the ponytail. And don't ask us curly gals what *we* think of humidity.

If you've chosen a skilled professional, he or she is most likely going to get real with your goals. It's not to bring you down and sabotage your dream of making over your look and your life. It's to temper your expectations and help you find what works best for you in your life. Sure, a professional stylist can make dark, curly hair sleek, straight, and light (or the other way around), but they should also arm you with information about what it takes to create that same style at home. What's the maintenance, the upkeep, the cost? You might need to know how to protect processed hair that will need heat to tame it, how a round brush and hair dryer on the highest setting are essential for that new style's curve and lift, or how often you'll need trims to maintain the overall look and health of your hair.

Always remember that you are your most valuable investment. You're going to hear that a lot in this book, and it definitely applies here. Notice that word *investment*. It's about time, money, and other precious resources. I'm not saying to break the bank here, but let's make decisions from informed places, because a makeover *is* an investment.

Maybe your transformation involves only a small change, like cutting off a couple of inches from your hair but keeping the same color and honoring your texture. All good and fine. But maybe it's more. And that's also fine—as long as you understand what your choice entails. Assuming you don't mind the work, upkeep, and new skill set you'll have to employ to recreate the photo you marched in with, then I say go for it!

Step #3: Take the Leap

You have spent time researching and found the right person to help make it happen. You've taken the plunge, made the appointment—armed with your sheaf of images—and consulted your stylist. And then, a couple of hours later, voilà! A different person is staring back at you in the massive, perfectly illuminated salon mirror.

Now what?

Lunch.

With your blood sugar levels back to normal, you've likely looked at yourself in your car's rearview mirror for the hundredth time. You're either incredibly proud of your new beauty-from-the-outside-in approach or scratching your lightly hair-sprayed coif and not quite sure yet. Either way, can I commend you for your leap of faith? I know this decision wasn't taken lightly, and you went there. Whether you like the look or not, you taught yourself something incredibly valuable about yourself, and the lesson will continue in ways you never dreamed imaginable.

A Fascination with Transformation

The right hairstyle can take years off your face—and so can the right makeup and application. That's next on the beauty-from-the-outside-in list. And with so much content available online, finding helpful guidance in this area has never been easier. Many beauty vloggers have become famous and wealthy on YouTube, and their experience and advice are readily available. But it's important to be aware of which guidance is best suited to your needs.

Beauty vlogging started with millennials demonstrating the latest looks to their peers. When I landed on this platform, in fact, there were very few women in their prime providing content to other women in the same age group. Thank goodness this has changed. It's hard for a more mature woman to relate to a twentysomething who doesn't have hooded eyes or a wrinkle to be found. Relatability is key, and I'm happy to say there is now content available that women of all ages can relate to.

Two of my more popular tutorials are titled "'Eye Lift' Makeup for Hooded, Heavy or Downturned Eyes" and "The Makeup Facelift." Why do these resonate with so many? Because women of all ages appreciate the power of makeup and its beautiful use of shade and light to change shape, size, and proportion.

I have always viewed makeup as an art, and I so appreciate the artistry of makeup masters like the late Kevyn Aucoin, who could transform celebrities and everyday people into something otherworldly. I featured Aucoin's book *Making Faces* early in my channel as a great source of inspiration when it comes to my own makeup technique.[3] I love the fact that every day I get to start as a blank canvas and then leave my bathroom as a piece of work—the good kind, of course! All kidding aside, it's a fascination with transformation that keeps me in my bathroom chair in front of my Hollywood mirror as the minutes tick by. I've seen what the right makeup can do. I know that when it complements a flattering hairstyle, it can leave a woman floating on a cloud and make her feel invincible.

The use of makeup dates back at least as far as the ancient Egyptians around 4000 BC. Both men and women are pictured in tomb drawings with dark kohl around their eyes, a signature of the Egyptian look. Makeup to enhance appearance and protect the skin was so relevant in this society that people were actually buried with makeup tools in their leather pouches. Can you imagine if there had been a Sephora around back then?

Style Lessons

Growing up in the 1980s gave me a great entrée into the world of makeup. Heavy eyeliner like that of the Egyptians was popular, coupled with rosy cheeks and super-red, glossy lips. (Hello, Pat Benatar!) Prince's "U Got the Look" and Robert Palmer's epic music video for "Addicted to Love" had us all addicted to the look.

When I started using makeup myself, I learned quickly to dial it up, and this over-the-top approach to makeup was a wonderful way to start. Less wasn't more in those days; more was more. On display were incredible music video icons and infamous supermodels with full-on glam to be emulated by us mere mortals. Believe me, I took notes.

As a hair and makeup enthusiast, I was the first to volunteer my time to gussy up my girlfriends before dances and proms.

They would come over, and I would tease their hair as high as it would go. ("The higher the hair, the closer to God" was the saying in those days, especially in Texas.) I widened and opened their eyes with the right shadow, liner, and mascara and glossed their lips to pouting perfection. That usually left me only ten minutes or so to get myself ready, but I took so much pride in my girlfriends' responses to their new looks that it didn't matter.

One Halloween my good friend Marisa's younger brother wanted a great costume to wear to school. I volunteered to spend the night at their house and then get up at six in the morning to spike the little guy's hair, slick down the sides, spray paint the tips of his killer mohawk in blue, and paint some stripes on his face. His sister and I accompanied him to his elementary school that morning, and he arrived to cheers and "Oh, my Gawd!" responses. That was a feather in my cap.

I also took a fashion-design class at Memorial High School and learned how to cut patterns and make my own clothes. A classmate and I designed and sewed our own outfits for our final project. My friend made these cool harem-style pants with slits that fit her tall, dancer-like frame to a tee. I went for an asymmetrical bias-cut dress in navy blue with stripes—something a news anchor might have worn in the day. We both made As and got featured in a large photo for our class yearbook.

In college at the University of Houston, I landed a coveted internship at CNN's *Style with Elsa Klensch* show. From 1980 to 2001, this program featured designers and runway shows from all over the world. When I started in January 1990, I was ready and eager to learn the inner workings of the fashion-meets-television world. My days would start by riding the train from my parents' home in Connecticut to Grand Central Station; then I'd take the subway for a few stops and walk a handful of blocks to my new work address. I would photocopy and file articles from *Women's Wear Daily* until Elsa returned from interviewing, say, Donna Karan or some French designer. Then I would "log the tape," which meant typing every question and answer verbatim. The accents of some of these international designers complicated things, but my fingers moved fast, and I quickly became at least somewhat proficient in deciphering broken English.

That job wasn't exactly glamorous. I did my share of coffee runs and dry-cleaning drop-offs for the show's host. But all the gofer work was worth it when I got to go backstage during New York Fashion Week and watch some of the shows, including Ralph Lauren's. I will never forget seeing Christy Turlington and Naomi Campbell chatting while standing next to a tall table. Christy snacked on a petite appetizer from a tray next to her while they animatedly exchanged life's goings-on.

These young supermodels were practically goddesses back in the day, deeply admired by fashion-conscious teenage and twentysomething girls like me. We had no social media to follow back then, no posts to like or messages to send, just pages of *Vogue* magazine to plaster on our walls and closet doors. I was awestruck, seeing these beauties in the flesh.

After the runway show, where I was mesmerized by the clothing and the models, I witnessed Christy and Naomi, along with Cindy Crawford and Linda Evangelista, happily hail a cab and hop in. They acted just like any other civilians in New York, although they did slide in with an angelic grace and elegance only possible after years on a runway and in front of a lens.

Learning by Doing

My longtime love of makeup, hair, and style—and the time I've devoted to making it work for me—has served me well. I wound up in a career where the proper use of all of the above was essential to conveying professionalism. Makeup for television is markedly different from makeup in real life, of course. The lights and cameras cut right through it, leaving a normally made-up face looking downright naked on TV. If you look almost like a streetwalker in real life, you'll nail it on camera!

Having to do more taught me how to apply more; how to contour in bone structure that wasn't there in my early years; how to "lift" my naturally hooded, German-side-of-the-family eyes; how to choose lipstick shades that wouldn't distract from what I was saying. As I worked, I began to perfect a method that would segue well to the YouTube platform.

Now, you're probably saying, "Wait a minute. You work in TV—you must have had *someone* doing your makeup!" Unfortunately, the makeup fairy never arrived at my place of work, and for that I'm eternally grateful. My colleagues and I had to figure it out all on our own—hair, makeup, wardrobe, you name it. Consultants came through on occasion to serve as guidance counselors of a sort, but ultimately it was up to us to get it right.

I remember binge-watching the Netflix political thriller *House of Cards* a few years after it was released in 2013. The character of Claire Underwood, played by Robin Wright, struck me as the perfect epitome of a classy professional woman; she exuded poise, class, elegance, and simplicity. When I first saw that character, I experienced a refining of my lens. I drew inspiration from the way her character was styled on the show and infused elements of it into my own signature look.

I learned how to dial it way up for work, and as I got older, I learned how to dial it way down in a normal daily setting. Less makeup works better as we age. I may still go through the same stages of what I apply, but my hand isn't as heavy.

Your Face Is Your Canvas

How does all this translate to you? Simple. It's a choice to sit yourself down in front of your makeup mirror and play. The variety of makeup available these days is astounding—there's something in every shade in multiple formulas adapted to every woman's need and available at almost every price point. As you've seen on my channel, you can achieve quite a sophisticated or simple makeup look using only drugstore products that won't break the bank. You can also choose to spend more money and experience the richness in tone and application that comes with more high-end products. There's something for everyone.

I want you to see this creativity in the same way an artist views a blank canvas. I want you to see the value in spending time to figure out what you like best—how to apply it and how to incorporate something new. You took an amazing leap when it came to your hair. You've seen how transformative makeup application can be. Imagine marrying the two.

One thing I've learned from my viewers is an overwhelming eagerness to try and learn. They see something they like, and they want more—more instruction, more guidance, more example. Just look at the amazing array of makeup tutorials out there. You have no shortage of self-made makeup artists willing to impart wisdom from their walk. It's an incredible and intimate opportunity for you to give good face. If you need some quick-start guides, search the Makeup Tutorials category on my YouTube channel. I have a wide array of looks and how-tos.

And let's not forget about skin care. That's been an important lesson for sun-loving gals like me. After those '80s shake-and-bake beach sessions came the '90s spots that just got darker and darker, along with the crow's feet. We paid a hard price, but thankfully there are many treatments to reverse the sun damage of our yesteryear. Skin care has evolved as beautifully as you have. There are many natural, effective products formulated without harsh chemicals, animal testing, or names you can't pronounce.

Also, I don't step outside anymore without mineral- and zinc-based SPF products, and I wear a hat for any prolonged exposure to the sun. I deeply hydrate my skin now with face oils, and I've relied on my smart-as-a-whip dermatologist to incorporate the big guns—prescription-strength retinoid and glycolic acid—into my skin care routine. I've been using those daily for more than a decade, and I can honestly say these shifts in my regimen have given me better skin in my early fifties than I had in my early forties!

Adjusting the Lens

At this point, of course, we've only touched on the beauty-from-the-outside-in changes that can get us started on a journey of transformation. Hair and makeup can make a big difference, but so can a new outfit or even a new pair of glasses. (We will look at the impact of wardrobe in a later chapter.) But whether it's hair, makeup, skin care, or style, there's no denying the power of an external transformation to kick-start change.

Paying attention to your look can send shockwaves through your system, alerting it that there's more to come. The outside-in approach to beauty isn't for other people's perception of you, but for your interpretation of you and how much you're willing to explore. This is sending a signal deep inside that there's bigger work happening here, a shift in mindset that the beauty you're cultivating on the outside is taking root and will lead to a shift in your overall being.

What I want to convey is my hope that this book—and this chapter in particular—will help you adjust the lens with which you are viewing your life. I want to help you bring things into focus.

When I think about adjusting my own life lens, I think about when I am composing a photo and choosing where I'm going to place the focus. What's the true subject of the photo? When you think about your life, are you focusing on the things that really matter to you? Or are you instead placing that focus (and your precious time) on things that are less important to you in the big picture of your life? I hope this book can be a valuable tool for you to sharpen that focal point, create intentions around what matters most to you, and then take action toward creating the life you want most.

TWO

. . . .

YOU ARE YOUR MOST VALUABLE INVESTMENT

ONCE YOU BEGIN TO PUT time and energy into improving yourself, something magnificent happens. It's contagious, infectious, and empowering. After spending a little more time on yourself and witnessing the powerful results, you'll think, *Why stop here?* After taking even one small step in one area of your life, you'll immediately want to take steps in other areas too.

Let's say you've taken my beauty-from-the-outside-in advice and made some changes to your hair or your makeup. Now you look more polished and refined, and you feel great about it. Next you start to wonder why your personal space is such a mess—such untidiness doesn't really reflect this person you're becoming. You decide it's time to get more organized, and you start working toward that. Or maybe it's time to tackle any extra weight that's been holding you back from your goal of getting healthy on the inside and seeing the benefits on the outside. Then the old clothes don't fit anymore, so there's an opportunity to spruce up your wardrobe and make better choices that reflect this new woman you're becoming.

Do you see how it works? With each new revelation comes new discoveries and interests, new opportunities to learn and grow, new possibilities for the future. This process is like compounding interest. The reinvestment in yourself leads to something even greater. Your value in your own eyes increases.

And no, the process of self-investment is *not* selfish. In fact, it's what makes it possible for you to be truly unselfish. Because your account is full, you'll be able to pay out increases. You'll discover new joy in giving because you actually have something to give. You're not in a deficit anymore, not depleted and in the red. And it all started by believing you're *worth* the time and money and effort to improve yourself.

Let's face it. It's easy to get lost in the shadows of depletion, sometimes out of necessity, neglect, or loss. It can happen like a slow buildup of dust, and before you know it, your brilliance and shine are coated with residue. That luster you once had is no longer there. You yearn for it and feel far removed from your natural brilliance. You see yourself as stale, tarnished, and old.

A viewer wrote in about a time when she felt this way. After a period of terrible loss in her life—a failed marriage and the death of a parent—her life seemed to be crumbling around her. Then one day she happened to be on YouTube and idly searched for a tutorial about making up hooded eyes. One of mine popped up, and she gave it a go. Even in the midst of her despair, she was able to tap into a deep, hidden desire to enhance her beauty.

She started receiving compliments on how she was applying her eye makeup. And soon she was making other changes in her life and experiencing a boost in her mental state. She wanted me to know that my message of self-care did lead to her feeling bold and blessed, and for that she was truly thankful.

This viewer could have easily succumbed to the emotional fallout from her hardships. But her choice to make small changes instead of losing herself in her grief proved to be a fork in the road. A makeup tutorial may seem pretty inconsequential after what she had been through, but her letter personifies what I'm here to preach: even if it's just to see yourself differently to feel better in the moment, *you* are worth it!

A Cosmic Wormhole Back to You

Given that all the work I'm encouraging you to do hinges upon your ability to believe that you are a valuable investment, I want to spend some time in this chapter helping you buy in to that belief. It's not always as easy as just saying it out loud and believing it. Many women have sidelined their own needs and desires for so long that they've lost touch with who they really are and what they really need. It takes a bit of effort for them to lay down everything else long enough to prioritize themselves.

So often we define ourselves by what we do instead of who we are. I can say I'm a mom, a daughter, a content creator, an author, and so on, with all of these roles constituting areas of work in my life. But who am I *really*?

If you're having trouble answering that question, you might try this simple little exercise. Find a quiet space where you won't be interrupted. Then cast your mind back to when you were about six years old and try to remember what you were like back then.

It might help to imagine asking yourself some specific questions. (I suggest speaking them aloud or writing them in a journal or notebook.) Stretch your memory and your imagination as you ponder how six-year-old you might answer these questions:

- What do you love to do?
- What *don't* you like to do?
- What are you good at?
- What is hard for you to do?
- What makes you angry or afraid?
- What gets you excited?
- What makes you happy?

If you like, you can write the answers down in a journal or on a device, or just close your eyes and think about them. It's okay if you're not sure about the answers or have trouble remembering. Chances are they will become clearer as you repeat the exercise.

This exercise is sort of like a rewind to the beginning of your life. It's a mental exercise designed to reconnect you with the powerful, positive emotions you felt as a child, when you allowed your true self to lead the way. Think of it as a journey back in time, a kind of cosmic wormhole that takes you back to the you that was meant to be.

What do you see when you take that imaginative journey and visualize yourself as a child? What lit your fire as a little one? Did you dabble in art and music, or were you more of an athlete? Did you love being in big groups or prefer your alone time? Were you tough or more sensitive? Were you a big-picture thinker, or did you enjoy focusing on the details of life? How did you feel about yourself?

By allowing yourself this quiet time to go back and suspend all of your current "reality," to quiet the naysaying voices that you might have listened to for years, you are beginning your transformation. By teaching your mind to release any self-limiting beliefs you may have formed as an adult—any insecurities, any stories you've been telling yourself about who you are—and adopting the mind of a child, you are "resetting." In the process, you are getting to know the real you better.

Let me give you an example. You may have an impression about me based on what you've seen or heard about what I do, but who I am might surprise you. I'm definitely an ambivert, meaning I'm both introverted and extroverted. While I come across as very social—and I am to a large degree—I'm usually one of the first to want to leave a party because of overstimulation. I have a cap on how much chatter I can handle. I much prefer one-on-one connection to large groups, and I covet my quiet and alone time. I'm also a deep thinker about big-picture ideas. I love to ponder the "whys" of life. Superficial conversation bores me, and I need artistic expression to feel connected to myself.

I also need nine hours of sleep to function well. I need to hear and see nature. I love and admire beauty in all forms. I have an innate desire to strive for excellence in everything I take on. I'm more tough than sensitive. I seem to have more "manly" qualities in terms of behavior, although I love to celebrate the "girly" in me.

In other words, I'm a study in contrasts. A true Gemini. And guess what? That was me at age ten, and it's still me today! Acknowledging this is "who I am" greatly influences what I do and how I invest in myself.

This tool, sort of a cosmic wormhole back to you, is something you can use again and again. You can repeat the exercise anytime life begins to feel overwhelming or you simply need to gain some perspective on who you are and what you want. It can help you rise above your circumstances, transcend your current reality, and have a vastly different emotional experience so that you can stay on this transformative path and not be deterred. The next time any voice in your head tries to convince you that you shouldn't be spending time on improving how you walk through life, just take a trip through the cosmic wormhole to remind yourself that you are worth it.

What's Holding You Back?

Sometimes to move forward, we have to release the past, the emotional chains that bind and limit our mobility. Without even realizing, we can use situational circumstances, bad choices, or being wronged as stumbling blocks to our success. So, in these quiet "me" moments, we may have to dig deep and do some serious analyzing of what's preventing us from living the life we desire.

For me, this dig-deep process started in my twenties. In those days I struggled in two critical areas of my life: my choices in men and my weight. And I would soon learn that those two areas of struggle were connected. As I have shared in a YouTube video called "My Health, Wellness and Weight Loss Journey," my path to addressing them was a gut-wrenching, emotional one, as it is for many women I know. I made the video because I felt it was important to show other women that they're not alone and that there is a way out of such struggles.

Although lean as a child, I grew heavier in my late teen years, and this trend carried over into the next decade. I now know I was addicted to carbs and sugar, plain and simple. I loved all food, even healthy food, but I gravitated toward those serotonin-releasing, nonsatiating choices for a reason.

I also tended to make certain choices when it came to men—cute guys who were also projects. I loved to pluck them out of the crowd—you know, the ones who looked good on the outside but were a little broken on the inside. I just knew they had great potential, and I was going to help them become all they were created to be and then some. In return I would gain their love and they would see my value.

As I'm sure you've guessed, none of this worked for me. After a series of failed long-term relationships and Weight Watchers and Jenny Craig diet-plan trials, it was time to get to the root of the problem. I sought therapy and quickly learned that who and what we are today often has roots in the emotional makeup of the six-year-old inside of us.

My six-year-old self was a playful and happy child, but she also felt an emptiness that no maternal attention or material objects could buy. I needed my father, and my father was often absent—sometimes physically and definitely emotionally. When I was young, he typically worked two weeks on and two weeks off at sea, and sometimes he would be gone for months. When he returned, his affections were clearly directed toward my mother, and I still felt a palpable absence and disconnect.

My father was old-school German, and he saw his role as that of a provider. He undoubtedly loved me, but he just wasn't a dad who would get down on the floor and play with his kid. My mom did her best to make up for the lack. She was present, involved, and very loving. But the relationship a daughter has with her father can often define her relationships later in life—not only with other people but with herself.

I learned in therapy that my eating issues were connected with feeling unworthy of my dad's affection. I had a hunger to be valued and loved and was driven by my desire to prove my worthiness to others, specifically men. Deep down I believed I had to earn their affection—that simply being me wasn't enough.

Cue the food. Although obviously necessary for life, it can also work as a drug, providing instantaneous changes in brain chemistry—moments of intense pleasure followed by moments of deep regret and withdrawal. I was using food that way, medicating the pain from my past. Couple that with a desire to rescue wounded puppies (men), and you have a recipe for an unhappy and unfulfilled existence.

A Bold Move Forward—and Back

When my therapist recommended that I write a letter to my dad, my eyes bulged. He quickly said, "You don't have to send it. Just get all your thoughts and feelings down on paper, then release them and yourself. Once you've done that, you can choose whether to send the letter or not."

I went home that afternoon and started writing. At first my pen hovered above the blank pages as I thought about where to start. And then, just as a sprinkle of rain turns to a torrent, my first tentative words became an outpouring. Tears fell onto the pages as I purged my soul of my pain and longing.

Many pages later, I finally stopped, then went back to read and reread my truth. Okay, there it was. I had released my emotions. But I wasn't satisfied. I folded my letter, stuffed the pages into an envelope, wrote the address, and licked the stamp, and off that letter went.

Then I panicked. *Dear God, what have I done?* But days went by with no call from my dad. *Did he get it? Has he read it? What if he never wants to speak to me again? What if I've made things worse?* You can probably imagine a twentysomething's thought process here. But I refused to second-guess myself. I had made a big, bold move to free myself, knowing that letter was for me and not for him. It was my self-investment. I had to remain confident in that choice.

The therapist had said that my dad might not understand or receive my letter well, but that writing it was about my release, a way to get past certain choices that weren't serving me. The best-case scenario would be a new pathway to my father, but there was no guarantee that scenario would take place.

It didn't, at least not right away.

I finally decided to call my father, and he answered the call with a chill in his voice. I was pretty sure he had read the letter.

After the obligatory hello, he confirmed that he had, then proceeded to talk. I sat there in silence, listening and feeling a queasiness take over, then an enormous sense of regret, then anger. For thirty minutes my father explained his childhood, insisting that *I* didn't understand *him* and his past, the hardships he had faced. There was no apology, no "I understand." Just a lecture.

A Journey of Healing

When we hung up, those crazy, wild tears made their way out again. I speed-dialed my therapist, and our next session was all about that call. The therapist sat and listened, expressing empathy for the wounded daughter in front of him. In that moment I felt heard, but not by the person I wanted to truly hear me. And now things were worse than ever. *How do I get past this?* I wanted to know. *How do I warm the frozen tundra that now defines the relationship between me and my father?*

The answer was simple although certainly not easy.

I forgave.

I know. You may be thinking, *How in the heck did you do that?*

It wasn't instantaneous. In fact, it took a while. But it did happen. Once I had come to terms with this source of pain in my past, I was able to consciously release the bitterness and anger that resulted from it. Gradually I began to see my dad as someone who had done his best with his skill set. Maybe he wasn't the warmest or most attentive father, but he excelled in other areas, and I learned to give praise and thanks for that. He was a Renaissance man, rich with experience and knowledge. There was never a question he couldn't answer. I finally decided to stop holding his failures and shortcomings against him. He couldn't change the past. Neither could I. I could only hold out hope that our future could look brighter and feel more loving.

As years went by, our weekly calls to stay in touch grew longer and more meaningful. My parents had divorced when I was in my midtwenties, and eventually my father met and married the most lovely and loving woman, who I believe truly softened his heart in his later years. He began to say "I love you" at the end of every call with genuine warmth and affection. I could feel the chains falling from my heart and my heart being washed anew. During one of the most difficult times in my life, when I was going through a divorce with my son's father, my dad and my stepmom came and stayed with me. My dad rose to the occasion, providing strength, encouragement, and invaluable support.

We also had traditions we developed through the years. Thanksgiving was always his favorite holiday. He'd cook his bacon-wrapped turkey, cabbage, stuffing, and potatoes and would then bake his *puffer*, a German pound cake. (I salivate just thinking of this feast.)

I even featured my dad in a YouTube video baking the cake and sharing the recipe with viewers. (You can search for it under the title "How to Make a German Pound Cake with My Dad!") Anyone watching that video would never know about our past relationship struggles. All that's visible is a genuine, loving family tradition and a mutual appreciation between the two of us. And my dad's thick German accent—that's just the icing on the cake!

My father left this world on April 4, 2016. As my stepmom and I helped him on this passage, I couldn't help but feel peace, even through the palpable pain of letting him go. Would I have been able to do that if I had not done what I did some twenty-five years before? If he had left this world while I was still filled with anger and resentment? That was not how I had wanted this story to end—and it didn't. Though I never heard my father say, "I'm sorry," I did feel the shift in the way he treated me, and maybe that was his way of saying it. He was a proud man who did, after all, truly love his daughter to the very end.

A New Relationship with Food and Exercise

What did all that have to do with the way I saw food—and men? That, too, was a gradual process that began with writing the letter to my father. Over time, as I worked through my feelings and tried to make different choices, I experienced a shift in the way I saw food.

Back when I was in college at the University of Houston, my best friend Monsour and I would often drive straight to Wendy's after class, and I'd order large french fries with a large Frosty— you know, that frozen chocolate cup of heaven! At least that's how I thought of it then. That would be my first meal of the day, and I'd follow it up with a trip to TCBY, the frozen yogurt store, where I'd order a large waffle cone dipped in white chocolate and sprinkles and filled with vanilla yogurt. I would purchase a cookie sandwich to go. Later, at home, I'd have a full dinner. And after all that I would beat myself up about those terrible food choices and what they were doing to my body. It was a vicious cycle of eating and then feeling bad about what I had eaten.

I didn't know it then, but I was using all those carbs, especially sugar, as an addictive substance—to raise the serotonin levels in my brain, triggering my pleasure sensors to give me a taste of happiness. I thought I was simply satisfying my cravings and savoring the flavor, though I would punish myself later for the lack of self-control. But my weight gain and the acne flare-ups on my upper back and shoulders were the telltale sign of my addiction.

I was confident and capable in other areas of my life. I generally made good choices; I was work-focused and determined. But that unaddressed black hole of unhappiness was undermining not only my health but the quality of my relationships with myself and others. It wasn't until I dealt with it that I began to experience true emotional healing. And that healing helped remove the emotional component behind my food choices. Finally, I was able to see food for what it really was and wasn't. It wasn't my dad's love, and it couldn't heal my heart. It could, however, fuel me and make me healthy, energized, and strong.

As my heart started to heal through self-knowledge and forgiveness, my connection with food shifted from emotional to physical. I studied what food does in the body and what it means to be truly healthy. I researched ways that certain foods can help prevent disease. I learned about inflammation in the body and how reducing it through diet and exercise can greatly increase one's chances of living a long, healthy life. I discovered that the right foods made me feel better than I could have ever imagined and enabled me to be stronger in my workouts. And, yes, I committed to those workouts.

Over time this new approach to food and exercise changed both my body and how I see it. These days I don't diet, and I don't have a battle with how I look. My approach to food comes from a balanced viewpoint of health and wellness. To me food is medicine, food is fuel, and, yes, food is a joy. I love healthy food as well as the occasional treat. But choosing what to eat isn't a war that rages in my head anymore. I don't have that angel on one shoulder and devil on the other battling it out.

In the same way, my approach to exercise isn't a joyless slog. Yes, there are days when I don't relish the idea of a workout. But in general, exercise is my release and my acknowledgment that God designed us to move. I feel better when my blood is oxygenated and my muscles are pumping, and the high lasts long after the workout is done.

As my relationship with my father improved and my body evolved to a place of harmony, I also experienced a shift in my relationships with men. Gradually I came to see myself as worthy just the way I am. Worthy of love. Worthy of acceptance. Worthy of happiness. Worthy of trust and commitment. My self-esteem rose from making positive choices in my life. Emotional freedom came later in life, but it came like a whitecapped, flowing river.

God's timing, you see, is always perfect. He knows when we're ready, but He also expects us to do the work needed to be ready. I had hurdles to overcome before I could embrace His goodness.

I've shared this deeply personal journey in the hopes that you can connect with it. No two stories are alike, but for most of us, there is a deep-seated connection between what has happened to us, how we responded, and the decisions we make in our present lives.

What roadblocks stand in your way that are keeping you from God's glory? Maybe now is a good time to tackle those so you can be free to live your blessed life. Maybe now is the perfect time to make that investment in you.

Should you seek therapy the way I did? Only you can answer that. My own time in therapy really helped me understand my past and the ways it was influencing my present life and behavior, often without my knowledge. It turned out to be a crucial part of investing in myself. But I'm clearly not a counselor or a therapist myself. So, for the purposes of this book, I'd like to suggest some simple and fun ways to help you get in closer touch with the *you* you're investing in. I think you'll find these valuable whether or not you decide to seek professional help.

A Vision for a New You

Perhaps it's been so long since you spent time on yourself that you don't even know who you are anymore, and you don't have a clue where you want to go with your life. Perhaps you have a vague vision of a better life but no idea how to achieve it. Or perhaps you're just looking for a fun way to stay on track with the changes you are already making.

If you're looking for more clarity, inspiration, and focus, I suggest creating a vision board—actually *two* vision boards: a passion board and a talent board. This exercise gives you something to meditate on and is the perfect follow-up to tossing all of that emotional baggage. As a visually driven person, I find it helps me home in on where I've been, where I'm going, and what matters most to me. It can also serve as a regular reminder that keeps me on course.

A classic vision board is simply a large piece of cardboard or foam board where you post pictures, quotes, words—anything that helps inspire you or keep you focused. But you don't have to stick with the classic. There are many different ways to create a visual inspiration. You can fill a blank journal with images and ideas, create a Pinterest page, or sign up for an app that gives you a place to post images.

I describe one of my favorite approaches in a video titled "Setting 2020 Intentions Using the Box Method." I've found it a creative way to meditate on what matters to me in a new year. I look for images that represent my intentions for the coming year and then clip or paste them onto a decorative box. I write letters to myself monthly as a means of checking in with my progress, and I keep those letters in the box.

What's Your Passion?

In this book you're embarking on a life-resetting journey that will require you to spend some time getting reacquainted with yourself. To help you do this, I recommend you start by creating a passion board (or journal, or computer board, or box). It's an exercise that can conjure up some strong emotions because you'll be analyzing where you are on your path to you, and it's possible you'll find you're on a dirt trail with snakes and tarantulas that bears no resemblance to the fruitful trail you've envisioned. But the very process of creating the board can help you move in the right direction.

The word *passion* is one of my favorites because it is the seed that bears the largest, ripest fruit. Your passions are simply what you care about most in life, what you love doing, what is meaningful to you at a deep level. They may have been with you from childhood, or they may stem from new discoveries. Wherever they come from, they're more than trivial interests or pastimes. They have the power to engage your heart and your soul. True passions energize you.

What kinds of interests and activities meet these criteria in your life right now? Start scouring your mind and heart and write them down as they come to you. There's no limit. You could have a long list or a short one. We all have passions, and they are as unique as our thumbprint.

If you're not clear what your passions are, ask yourself some of the same questions you asked your six-year-old self during the "cosmic wormhole" exercise. What makes your heart sing? What do you care about most deeply? What gets you excited or sparks joy in your heart? What activities tend to take you to a place where time seems to fly by? What interests bring you energy or a sense of peace and rightness?

Once you have your list, read through it and consider how it makes you feel. Seeing this list of passions right in front of you should generate a certain warmth and excitement and be a window to your joy. Now let's bring that list to visual life by searching for images that represent your passions.

I almost always do my image search on the internet, but you can use magazines, brochures, even old books—whatever you have on hand. As you locate images that speak to you, cut them out, print them out, or paste them onto a blank page in an app and save them. Keep thinking, praying, meditating, and collecting. Search, seek, clip, repeat until you have a nice collection of images that represent your passions.

As you search, keep in mind that you might not be in a position to act on your passions right now, but you don't need to. What matters is for you to unleash your imagination sans limitations and find images that help you visualize your passions. You may even discover new passions in the course of your search. Add them to your collection.

My own passion board would contain images related to yoga and dance; music that fills my soul; intimacy; healthy food; writing; a camera and microphone; gardening; artistic expression; beauty; exercise; rest; a white sandy beach with turquoise water; travel; animals; fulfilling relationships; meaningful conversations; listening; being a good mom, wife, daughter; making a difference; and a connection to God. (I'm not listing these in order of importance. That's not necessary at this point. Just let the ideas flow.)

Along with the images, look for quotations that inspire you or write down what stirs you. Let your thoughts flow freely without the need to edit. It's important to read what you have to say about these passions—where are you most descriptive, yearning, hungry. What you write will reveal a lot about you, including things you aren't aware of.

Once you've amassed a significant collection of words and images, sort through them and pick the most evocative—the ones that mean the most to you and elicit your most powerful response. (Even this process will help you understand yourself better.) Now you're ready to make your board by assembling the images into a kind of visual collage.

If you are making a physical board, find or purchase a big piece of cardboard or foam board. Print out or cut out your images and paste, tape, or pin them to your board. If you are preparing an online version, a journal, a box, or whatever, simply adapt the process to your chosen medium. But however you choose to create your passion board, take your time and make it beautiful. I want you to enjoy the presentation of what you create because you'll be looking at this for a while!

What Do You Bring to the Table?

Once you feel complete here, it's time to move on to your talent board. This is where you're going to put images that reflect your gifts, talents, skills, and abilities—your tools for turning your passions into reality.

Again, start by making a list. And don't look at me with a blank stare. I know you have talents—many of them! You have also developed skills in a number of areas. Are you good with numbers, logic and reasoning, people, parenting, designing or creating beauty, cooking, playing an instrument, organizing, communicating, listening, teaching, leading, sales, creating businesses?

If the word *talent* intimidates you, think of what you have a knack for, what tends to come easy for you, or what skills you've developed over the years. What have other people told you you're good at? What do you think you might be good at if you tried? What personal resources could help you develop your passions?

You've probably cultivated such talents and skills over time in myriad ways. Even if they don't seem as if they will be "useful" in this journey, still include them. They are your tools for creating the life you want.

Maybe you tap into your talents daily, or maybe it's been a while since they've been allowed to come to the surface. Either way it's important to get real here. I want you to think of yourself as someone whom God has gifted with talent. He planted a seed in you. Maybe it hasn't been watered in a while, or maybe it's never been watered. That doesn't matter. There's no judgment here. There's no judgment anywhere in this book. I want to get you in a judgment-free zone in your life. It's one of the best gifts you can give yourself and anyone else.

So let your talent board soar. Look for images that represent your God-given gifts—those you have fiddled with somewhat and those that have been lying dormant. Make your board colorful, expressive, and authentically you.

You'll find that some of your talents—or many of them—will relate to your passion board. That's good. It means you have practiced developing some of your talents. Or maybe you're seeing an untapped talent somewhere. How exciting! You have a new potential endeavor to actualize.

Once you're done collecting images and words, do the same with them as you did for your passion board. Print out, clip, and attach them on a surface where you can refer to them again and again.

Once you've finished creating your two vision boards, place them in a spot where you can see them every day—your bedroom dresser, your refrigerator, the front door, somewhere in your office. The process of creating them will have helped you learn about yourself. But the process of referring to them regularly will help them change the way you think and even dream. Let the images and words that represent your passions and talents sink into your very soul. Let them remind you that you are worthy and capable of transformation. And let them be a source of energy and inspiration as you move forward.

This process of creating vision boards doesn't have to be a one-time exercise. You can return to it anytime you feel that you need a reminder that you are your most important investment.

Finding You

Passions and talents are funny and can reveal themselves at such surprising moments. Let me share a story from my youth that helped me realize a talent unbeknownst to me and gave me a hint to my future career. (Such "God winks" often appear if our eyes are open to them.)

It happened when I was thirteen. One of my best friends at the time invited me to go with her and her family to Nashville to see Michael Jackson and his brothers perform. Crystal's parents were friendly with the Gatlin Brothers, a famous country-music group, so we flew to Knoxville and stayed at Larry Gatlin's sprawling home in the countryside. Days of swimming and consuming Southern food were epically capped off on the night of the concert.

We traveled to Nashville in the Gatlin Brothers' tour bus like rock stars, feeling the buildup to what would eventually become not only a great time but a defining moment in my life. Good connections got us great seats on the floor, where for the next few hours we spun and danced our well-choreographed Michael moves to the point of sheer exhaustion. I remember vividly what I wore: a brown cotton jumpsuit with a wide belt. My brown curly hair was wild and free. (It was practically plastered to my face by night's end.)

Then something amazing and serendipitous happened when a local reporter started asking concertgoers what they thought of the show. The reporter approached us and spoke first to Crystal, who was far more outgoing than me. She answered the reporter's question a little hesitantly, obviously uncomfortable at having to do it on the spot, with a camera rolling.

Then it was my turn.

I don't remember doing this, but Crystal remembers vividly and shares the story to this day. Apparently, without premeditation, I grabbed the reporter's microphone, turned to the camera, and waxed poetic about what a great performance it was, how we came from Houston and danced in the aisles, and so on and so on, looking point-blank into the camera, not a fear or care in the world.

As the reporter moved on, my friend looked at me in disbelief. "That's what you're going to do for a living!" she said.

I came out of my trance. "Huh?"

And there it was—the moment when a hitherto unknown talent and passion came together for me.

Do you have any moments like that, that you can call upon? Any epiphanies, defining moments, calls of clarity? Any moments of Michael singing in your head?

Maybe it's not quite so dramatic. Maybe it's just a feeling you get when you're exploring one of your talents. How easily things seem to come. How good you feel in the moment. If we've lost sight of those reactions, it's up to us to sharpen that lens, to hone and reconnect.

I want you to do this here. Spend time. Don't rush. This is your life. You've been around for many, many years now. Rome wasn't built in a day, your vision boards shouldn't be either. Enjoy the process. Think of it as a tool for exciting discovery—a way of finding the "you" you want to explore, cultivate, and reinvent.

Or maybe you want to sharpen your lens in a new direction. Maybe the children are out of the house and you're at a pivotal moment in your life to start anew. Maybe one career ended abruptly—or simply faded out due to boredom—and it's time to go in a new direction. What will that look like? How will you get there?

I can say this: if you start from a place of passion, talent, and faith, all good things will come.

Give Yourself Grace

From experience, I know this vision board exercise can evoke unwanted emotions, including regret over paths not taken, talents unused, passions unexplored. Can I ask you to offer yourself grace in these moments? Sometimes we beat ourselves up for settling, resting, resisting, or not moving forward.

But you had your reasons. They could have been driven by past pain, financial necessity, fear, commitments, or simple practicality. Whatever they are, it's okay. And the beauty in this process is that it's never too late. You're never too old to grow.

Please don't get caught up in the judgment, whether self-imposed or laid on you by others. At any moment at any time in our lives, we have a chance to hit the reset button. It's the ultimate gesture of grace we can offer ourselves, aside from seeking forgiveness from God. One ask, one button push, and it's done. Erase the chalkboard (or the vision board!) and write anew. What an awesome gift!

To redirect and redesign your life, you must do two things: (1) analyze the past and see where you possibly sabotaged yourself, and (2) look for traits that served you well and can serve you in the future. The "cosmic wormhole" and vision board exercises I have described in this chapter can help you do this.

If you resolve to start anew out of a sense of dissatisfaction, you must resolve to do things differently in the future. But you also need to consider what has worked well for you and what you did that set you up for success. Let's find our strengths and celebrate those so that we can carry those behaviors forward.

Be sure to offer yourself gratitude for your accomplishments and a job well done. It's important to see ourselves in a positive light as we work to grow toward even more positivity. But let's also acknowledge areas that require more focus, effort, or intensity so that we can change those and write a new story.

Once you decide where you need to make adjustments, try not to get overwhelmed. You might look at your passion and talent boards and think, *Whew, I've got some serious work to do!* You can do it, but probably not all at once. It's a process.

Rediscovering the Physical You

If health, wellness, or spirituality-related words or images are on your vision board, might I encourage you to tackle those first? I've found that taking care of myself physically or spiritually leads to an enormous feel-good endorphin release. We are mental, physical, and spiritual beings. Yet we often deny ourselves the opportunity to explore all these areas equally because of fear (*I can't do that!*), prejudice (*That's just not me!*), time constraints, or simple lack of motivation.

I'm sure you've noticed how good you feel after a challenging workout, a deeply physical and meditative yoga class, or a long swim or walk. It's your body saying, *Yes, this is what I need. Give me more!* And mental clarity often goes hand in hand with intense physical exertion. It's as if we've cleaned the gunk out of our eyes and regained twenty-twenty vision. So if you're not seeing clearly right now, might I encourage you to move? Even a small change like a walk around the block can make a difference.

I could write an entire chapter on physical health and how it carries through to every area of our lives, from getting the brain juices flowing to sexual arousal to actually smiling at yourself in the mirror postmenopause! It's not only possible; to me, it's a requirement.

Focusing on our physical well-being becomes even more critical as we age. For women, menopause can bring hormonal depletion, bone loss, and emotional withdrawal. If we don't dig in our heels to physically right the ship, then we might shipwreck beyond repair. And if you're in a menopausal fog right now, I encourage you to seek options so you can live optimally. There are many ways to treat symptoms and obtain a better balance during this time of life. Suffering is so old-school, and you are not. I've done several videos with female doctors who specialize in menopause, and I'm here to say that the spotlight is shining brightly on this area of a woman's life—*finally!*

In addition to exercise, physical well-being also comes from eating the right kind of food. As I've mentioned, once I got over my emotional hang-ups, I started to see food differently. I made the conscious choice of learning what food does in the body, and I've experienced firsthand what an incredible assist it can give in achieving overall health and wellness. Simply put: you eat well, you feel well.

The specifics of what it means to eat well will vary and may take some experimenting. Some women do best with plant-based eating, some thrive on keto or Mediterranean diets, others feel best with a simple, balanced three meals a day. For me, living a healthy, clean life involves limiting my alcohol intake and cutting way back on sugar, flour, dairy—all the whites, basically. If you check out my "What I Eat in a Day" video, you'll see it's chock-full of produce, protein, lower-glycemic fruit, and healthy fats. This approach to eating leaves me feeling and looking in top shape, as my dad would say!

I'm also a big believer in intermittent fasting, blocking off periods of time when I don't eat at all. My particular approach is to have dinner at seven in the evening and not eat until eleven o'clock or noon the next day. By so doing I allow my body the chance to repair itself on a cellular level and to adjust my hormone levels to make stored body fat more accessible. This natural altering of the metabolic rate not only helps me burn more calories but also gives me incredible mental clarity. (I do a lot of my writing during this time.) According to many reports, fasting also has potential to help with insulin levels, heart health, cancer, even Alzheimer's. I do it because it has me functioning at my optimal best.

Exploring the Spiritual You

Faith and prayer play a huge role in self-investment.

What's going to see you through the tough times? The times when things aren't happening quickly enough or the change is not apparent enough? When your efforts to renew your life feel like all work with no reward? That's where faith comes in. For me, it's been a crucial aspect of my personal journey, which I will describe in more detail later in this book. For now, I just want to say that my connection to God has made all the difference in my life. I've come to depend on Him for wisdom and insight to guide my decisions, for comfort and strength to see the process through, for the patience to trust His timing, and for grace to handle my inevitable failures.

I don't know what I would do without the resources of faith and prayer, and I hope you will find ways to include those resources in your life as well. Otherwise, where will you derive your strength when that pint of ice cream is calling or when your spouse frowns upon your new pursuits or when you're just feeling your own weakness? Who will lift you in the moment and remind you that nothing good comes from complacency? I know who, and He is who I turn to again and again.

I can't say it often enough: *you* are your most valuable investment, and God is right there with you!

So now that you've identified your passions and talents, it's time to act.

THREE

· ·

BOLD AND BLESSED

YOUR AGE OR STAGE OF life has no bearing whatsoever on your ability to make bold moves and important changes. There is, in fact, no excuse for sitting on the sidelines or letting someone else call the shots in your life.

I always say I am my own compass; I set the course for my own life. I want to inspire you and implore you to do the same. That's what I mean by making your bold moves. I'm not talking about adopting a brash new personality or acting on impulse or on a dare. What I'm talking about is summoning the courage to choose positive change and to act on that choice when the time is right for you, even if you're not sure what the result will be.

I wouldn't be qualified to write this book if I didn't continue to share my own journey, but such transparency hasn't always been easy for me. I've had to work hard on *letting go*—two terrifying words for a control freak. And yes, I was a bona fide control freak. So learning to be real was a bold, risky move for me.

One of my biggest steps in choosing transparency came

when I was forty-seven. I was asked to be included in a new photography book called *Prime: Reflections on Time and Beauty*, by renowned photographer Peter Freed.[1] *Prime* profiled a variety of women in middle or late life, many of whom you'd recognize—sociologist Brené Brown, supermodel Christy Turlington Burns, and many other impressive women. I was enchanted with the use of the word *prime* to describe women in this age group—*my* age group. But my feelings were more complicated when it came to Peter Freed's planned approach to the photography.

Prime blazed a trail for full-on transparency in the beauty realm, meaning all the women were photographed with no makeup. This was well before the bare-faced look became a movement on social media and TV—and before I even had a presence on those platforms. I had no YouTube channel yet, no Instagram following.

So, would I accept the invitation to pose? A twentysomething or thirtysomething Dominique would have shot down the opportunity in a heartbeat. *What, go barefaced and have people see me as I truly am? Never!*

But I was a fortysomething Dominique when the opportunity arose, and by then I knew better. I made the choice to accept and was so glad I did. The photographs in that book turned out to be stunningly beautiful. And the profiles that accompanied them—stories of women coming to grips with what it means to be in their prime—were pure poetry.

I will share with you an excerpt of what I wrote for my page.

Hi, I'm Dominique Sachse: Houstonian, broadcast journalist, mom, daughter, friend, and former perfectionist. How's that one relevant? Simple. Breaking the chains of perfectionism, or the perceived reality of it, led me to my prime.

During my career warpath, I married and had a child, a beautiful boy who had a rough start coming into this world. Diagnosed with a milk-protein allergy, reflux, and colic, he rarely stopped crying, which meant there was no sleep for anyone. We all struggled for an eternity, and it pained me to see him suffer. I tried every remedy in the book, but to no avail. We just had to wait and offer comfort.

My marriage was also suffering during that time. This was the first time my perfect life wasn't so perfect, and it felt uncomfortable. While I was honing the skill of being real on air, somehow, I couldn't make it translate to real life. I kept my problems to myself for fear of bursting the perfect bubble. It's like putting the lid on boiling water. At some point it's going to blow, and I did.

Therapy 101. You can't fool the therapist. While you may try to fool yourself, they can see right through you. I was exposed as a perfectionist. My perfectionism had served me well in some parts of my life, but caused the demise of other parts. I had to deal with it. My marriage didn't survive. I had to go through divorce and single parenting in the public eye. This happens all the time, but it was my initiation into nonperfectionism. I couldn't take baby steps. I had to dive right in.

It was probably the best thing that could've happened. My forced entry into this reality was slowly making me a better person. I started revealing myself to my parents and friends in ways I hadn't before. It brought us closer. Protecting my son's emotions was priority one, and helping him through this transition became my new mission.

Somehow work was calming during this chaotic time of my life, and my personal turmoil was making me a better broadcaster. It was as if a shell had cracked. I've heard that now I'm more relaxed, empathetic, sympathetic, personable, and relatable.

So that stripped-down face you see on the opposite page wouldn't have happened a few years ago. She wouldn't have felt comfortable enough to do it.

Not perfect. To me that's what being in your prime is all about—learning to let go and truly live.

Agreeing to be profiled in Freed's book was a big and bold move in my life, an honor, truly, and an example of the risk-taking that has served me so well my entire life. Not only was it another nudge in my bold thinking; it was also a conscious choice that opened the gates to more fulfillment in both my professional and personal life. At that point I had already made big moves in terms of pursuing a career, but now I needed to be bold in choosing who I was going to be as a person. Being photographed for *Prime* gave me the opportunity to rid myself of the veil of perfection that didn't allow the real me to shine through.

I realized I was enjoying this new me, the real me. It was as if life exhaled. Maybe part of it was that I was approaching meno-pause and rounding the corner to fifty. And you know what often happens to women around that age? We stop giving a flip about a lot of things that once caused us a lot of grief and worry—such as other people's judgment!

That was definitely true in my case. But while part of me was metaphorically flipping the bird to the world, another part of me was becoming deeply interested in caring for a segment of it.

It was around this time that I started my YouTube channel and beefed up my presence on social media. I wanted my content to be meaningful, helpful, and relevant, stripped of any pretense for women over forty—a safe haven where they could share, compare, and, yes, go there! I also wanted it to include a spiritual component. My faith is my cornerstone, and not acknowledging its role on these platforms would be like not setting foundation with powder.

When I first started my YouTube channel in 2014, I studied other channels and other content creators, paying special attention to how they organized their information or portrayed their particular "brand" or "lane." One thing I noticed was that many of these people used a tagline, a catchphrase that they'd say at the end of every video. I felt inspired to do the same.

Since I was doing "lifestyle" videos, I felt my tagline had to be something that truly described my own journey and also paved the way for others. I spent some time considering my life path from childhood to the present moment. And what stood out to me was the power of my bold choices. Again and again I'd chosen to take a leap off the high diving board (metaphorically speaking). Every single leap had been scary as heck but always fruitful—and exhilarating. The fear in the pit of my stomach almost always turned into an undeniable high. And the confidence that leap created within me equipped me to jump even higher the next time and the time after that. Even my occasional belly flops helped move me forward because I chose to learn from them.

I could see the connection between my willingness to be vulnerable and bold and the resulting blessings that poured out afterward. Hence, my very own tagline was born: "Be bold and be blessed." I believe God whispered those words to me to permeate every woman's soul.

Here's one example of that. We all face different levels of challenges and obstacles in life. I received a letter from a woman who suffers from a medical condition that causes both physical and emotional pain. She has endured multiple hospital visits and broken bones as a result. Nevertheless, she believes she has been incredibly blessed with a husband, children, and a fulfilling career. She said that she had connected to my content because of something her mother often said: "No matter what cards life deals you, put on your lipstick and hold your head up high!" She was committed to doing that, even on her days of struggle and pain. That was clear in the photos she sent of her and her family. Not only is she physically stunning, but you can see a spark in her eyes of love, self-esteem, and giving it her all.

I was incredibly moved when I read that woman's letter. To me she is the epitome of what it means to be bold and be blessed. Her bold choices are part of the blessings she acknowledges so graciously.

When I read this beautiful woman's story and saw her photos, I could almost see that she drew a line in the sand. She could have easily defined herself by her condition and lived within its limitations. Instead, she obviously said to herself, *I deserve more. I am more than my disease. I want a family and career, and I'm going after it.*

Her choice to do just that is exactly what I mean by making bold moves.

I feel that risk-taking is like a light switch. It's off, and then with a flip, it's on, light and bright! Some light switches, of course, have dimmers to subtly adjust the brightness, and that may be nice for a room's ambience, but that's not what I'm talking about here. It's the full-on drastic difference from dark to light that risk-taking looks and feels like.

Now, that doesn't mean you should always leap without looking. I'm not saying you should just do what you want without planning and preparing. But there always comes a time when you've done what you can to prepare. You're right there at the edge, and all that's left is to jump. So, you jump. You flip the switch, and the light comes on. That's what it means to be bold.

Bold moves can be hard and sometimes scary, but they are necessary for growth and discovery. You'll know when it's time because that internal voice of yours will be stirring, pulling, suggesting, and sometimes screaming at you to flip that switch! It's your job not to talk yourself out of flipping it—because if you choose to stay there in the dark, you might miss out on some of the biggest and most exciting moments of your life, as well as the opportunity to learn a heck of a lot about yourself in the process.

The Faith Connection

When I think back to the bold moves I've made in my own life, I am always amazed to see how God's hand was guiding me. At the time I just believed I was operating on willpower combined with sheer luck. But now I realize the Presence was there, carefully crafting and orchestrating every move.

He will be there for you too. But don't expect Him to always spell things out for you. That's not how it usually works. In fact, often you won't understand exactly what is happening until you look back. But that doesn't mean He's not working in your life.

Making your bold moves (and reaping the blessings) means moving forward in faith—listening for God's guidance, keeping your spiritual eyes open for the opportunities He brings your way, preparing yourself the best you can, and then choosing to leap when the time seems right, even if you're not completely sure you're ready.

I can see all this so clearly now when I look back on my own life. Many of the opportunities I encountered were unprecedented. My boldness in taking advantage of those opportunities helped make them real. The rich details are where the blessings lie.

I was two years into a radio job, working as an evening disc jockey at Houston's Mix 96.5, which featured an adult contemporary format with hits from the '70s, '80s, and '90s. I got a call from someone I had worked with previously at Metro Traffic, where I had reported traffic conditions for a variety of radio stations. Since then, he had been doing the traffic reports on TV for KPRC Channel 2.

Here's how that conversation went.

"Hey, Dominique. It's Neil. I hear they're looking for a woman to do on-camera traffic reporting for the morning show instead of just having my voice over the traffic maps. I remember you saying you wanted to break into TV, and this may be the perfect opportunity. Interested?"

I almost dropped my headset. "Of course I'm interested!" I practically shouted before he'd even finished his sentence. So he put me in touch with the news director, and I followed up.

The year was 1993, and at that time Channel 2 News had two male newscasters, a male weatherman, and a male traffic voice. They were in serious need of some estrogen! It turned out they had already considered several women for the position, and while they all may have *looked* the part, there was one big problem: those women didn't know their freeways. The traffic broadcast uses chroma key technology, which means the reporter works in front of a green or blue screen where a map is superimposed behind them for reference. So that reporter had better know where everything is or she'll be pointing to the 610 Loop but talking about Interstate 45.

Fortunately, I knew Houston's freeways like the back of my hand, so I felt confident about my audition. Afterward I sat down with the news director, and the words he said next would change my life forever.

"Dominique, you're hired."

I didn't quite realize it at the time, but that was a first—and not just for me, but in the industry. The typical path to this type of position was to "pay your dues" and "develop your journalistic chops" with entry-level positions in smaller markets for years before you became an on-camera traffic reporter. I was young and a newcomer, with zero experience in television news. But I had the hunger, and I was determined to make that job work.

The rest of the news team wasn't so sure. In fact, they were extremely skeptical that I'd be able to make it. But despite the sideline chatter, I kept my head down and worked hard. I air checked myself regularly, pulled tape, and critiqued myself tirelessly. I knew this was a tremendous growth opportunity, and I was my own best and worst critic, constantly striving to improve in delivery, connectivity to the viewers, and appearance. I had to make bold moves on a daily basis, and I loved cultivating my new craft.

About one year into the traffic position, I was really jelling with the morning team. We were in a groove, and it felt good. Then when KPRC was sold and our upper management was sort of in flux, let's just say God breathed in my direction.

The acting news director called me into his office one afternoon. He told me one of the anchors was going on vacation soon. I had no idea where he was headed with this, so I just nodded and smiled. And then he hit me with, "I want you to fill in for him while he's away."

The wind was knocked out of me, but only for a second.

"You do know I've never anchored before," I replied.

"Yes. But I know you can do it."

"Well, okay then," I said, and then I think I floated out of his office, my feet barely touching the ground, yet with that all-too-familiar trepidation in the pit of my stomach. I couldn't believe it. I was going to fill in as coanchor on the morning news—in Houston, one of the top markets in the country. It didn't even seem possible.

That week, while sitting next to coanchor and longtime Houston news institution Bob Nicholas, something incredible happened. A breaking news story hit. A gas line ruptured and sparked what would become known as the San Jacinto River Fire. Flames were racing down the river, setting everything in its path on fire—houses, cars, mobile homes, you name it. And as I covered the story with no script, just flying by the seat of my pants, I discovered my true passion in this business—processing and interpreting information and then conveying it to viewers in a relatable and neighborly way.

It was a responsibility I didn't take lightly, speaking to the people being affected by this disaster and giving them vital information they needed so they could stay safe. *I want to offer compassion and understanding, without the armor, while maintaining professionalism and conveying the facts.* That one line right there is what has guided my entire news career.

Mind you, I never plotted a course in broadcast news, because at the time, the news was a male-dominated industry, hard and linear in scope and style. I grew up watching it but never saw myself in it. I had always assumed I would go the route of entertainment news, which was so much more personality and energy driven. Yet, there I was, sitting behind the desk, delivering the news, and still feeling true to myself.

People in key positions had seen my drive and the talent I'd started cultivating in radio (the perfect training ground to feel comfortable communicating without a script), and they had rolled the dice on me. Word has gotten back to me from multiple sources that my then general manager, Steve Wasserman, the man who hired me to become a full-time broadcast journalist, still says to this day, "My best move was making Dominique Sachse a news anchor." He did what no other manager had done back then, and I am forever in his debt. He took an enormous risk on a kid he believed in but who hadn't proved herself yet. Talk about a bold move on his part!

I share this because I have a big opportunity here to say, "Thank you, Steve!" He gave me the chance by opening the door. But I still had to make the bold move to walk through it.

My coanchor, Bob Nicholas, welcomed me from the start and was always supportive and encouraging. In fact, I came to call him Big Daddy, and he's still one of my nearest and dearest friends. One of the greatest lessons Bob taught me was to always remember that I am a part of the Houston community, not just a face on a TV screen. He would bring me along to charity events, where we'd emcee. I was his sidekick not only on set but also at a podium, where we'd lend our time to various causes.

While Houston may be an expansive city, it still has a small-town feel to it. That sense of connection is important here, more so than in other big news markets. I've always viewed myself as a representative of my community. That's still very much a part of who I am. Bob was there for me during an intense growth phase—successes, failures, and all. When I made a mistake, he'd pick me up and dust me off while still offering his sweet smile and words of wisdom. What a gift!

Bob was a friend, a confidant, and a mentor—all in all, a great TV husband. I've always said that anchor teams are like arranged marriages, and when you're paired with someone, you just hope and pray that it's a good fit. The viewer can smell a fake, but when the chemistry is right, it's magic! I'm blessed to have been paired with so many talented and diverse coanchors over the years. On-air talent feels like family, and that's everything to me.

The Right Bold Choice

People often ask me why I stayed in Houston. Why not move on to the bigger markets like Los Angeles or New York? Or why not network television? In my early career, in all honesty, that was exactly what I was going for. To me, Katie Couric's job on *The Today Show* was the perfect trifecta of hard-hitting journalism, in-depth interviews, and fun personal interest. I believed I had the personality and the skill set to pull off something like that, and I really would have liked to try.

But as time went by and my life changed, with a husband and a child and the need to balance being a present parent with growing my career, I found that staying put was an easy decision. In a sense, it was my next bold move.

I worked my way up the ranks, eventually settling into the prime evening slots of six and ten, where I've been anchoring since 2004. I've been honored to be part of the KPRC news team for many years now, and the great work we've done together has earned us multiple awards and honors in the industry—from Emmys to AWRT (American Women in Radio and Television) awards and the prestigious Edward R. Murrow award. We have a world-class team, and everything we do, from vision through execution, is a collaborative effort. We've made our bold moves together, and I'm deeply grateful to have been part of this news organization.

At the publishing of this book, I have closed the chapter on what has been an incredible twenty-eight-year ride in the local TV news business. I feel beyond blessed that Houston viewers welcomed me into their homes for more than a quarter century. But now it's time to make my next bold move—this book. I didn't want to rest on my laurels. I believe there is more for me to do.

Writing Your Own Tagline

Maybe you can relate to my story and have experienced professional success and satisfaction. Maybe you feel that you've been pedaling along but not really reaching your highest potential. Or maybe you've gotten off track somewhere and your life today is nothing like you had in mind. Wherever you are, you may be just one bold move away from getting back on track.

Wherever you are in life, wherever you've been or wherever you want to go, you have the chance to create your tagline. How will it read? What do you want it to say about you? It's one thing to identify your passions and talents; it's a whole other thing to use them to rewrite your own life script. That's where the boldness comes in. It really is a risk. It takes faith—and more.

As you can see, making your bold move is both a choice and an action. It's a collaboration between your logical and emotional state, where one is not driven by the other and all factors come into play—who you truly are as a person, where your strengths lie, what you know you're capable of, and how you feel about the pursuit and yourself in it. When you think of what might happen, does it conjure emotions of being satisfied, fulfilled, challenged, and complete? It's the perfect marriage of both sides of your brain working in tandem. It's pure honesty, not overridden by your subconscious or by the words of others.

Since I am visually driven, as I believe many of us are, I find it helps to actually visualize myself making a bold move. I recommend this to you as an exercise. When considering a risky move, imaginatively step out of your body and watch yourself do it. How do you look? What does your environment look like? This experience can almost be like floating through a vision board. As you do it, consider how you feel about yourself in this bold existence.

I did exactly that when I was about to start writing this book. I would visualize myself at the computer with the words just flowing effortlessly—a journalist's dream! Once I knew what that felt like, I would call upon that visualization time and time again if I ever had any doubt that I could fill a fifty-thousand-word book. Also, I can't tell you how many times I reflected on and visualized my previous bold leaps as I was preparing to make another one. For me, at least, the feelings that those visuals imparted provided me with a true kick start.

Most important, ask yourself the right questions about the moves you're ready to make. Consider the cost/benefit or risk/reward ratio. You want your bold moves to add value to your life, not take away from it. Remember, being bold is not the same as being thoughtless or foolhardy. A bold move has a better chance of succeeding if you count the cost.

Say, for example, you're considering a bold move that will require you to be less present with your family or children. If that sacrifice isn't worth it to you, then maybe now isn't the time. Or perhaps you will have to find creative ways to work around the issue. You might have to shift your schedule, get up earlier or stay up later, to make it all work. You may have to give up certain aspects in your life (TV or other less fruitful areas) to make time for this new exploration and discovery. Or perhaps you could enlist a spouse, a parent, or a friend to step in and pick up where you left off.

If you are in a relationship, making your bold moves will almost always require honesty and probably some negotiation. These situations call into play the solidarity and cooperation in the relationship as you find ways to honor both your commitments and your desire to move forward with your life. Change may be scary for those around you and will probably put a spotlight on the quality and health of your relationships.

I encourage you to be sensitive to those around you as you express your desire for change in certain areas of your life. Let them know that you would love for them to be on board, and offer ideas on how that can happen. Ask for the support you need, but reassure your loved ones that your transition is all part of making you happier and more fulfilled, which will also make you better in any role in which you serve.

If there's ever any struggle in this area, that's what pastors and counselors are for. No one ever said risk-taking decisions would be easy or without consequence, but you certainly don't want to enter into something without proper consideration.

Practicing Boldness

Not all bold moves are big and scary, of course. And practicing boldness in little ways is a great way to prepare yourself for bigger bold moves when the time is right.

For instance, what is one thing you could do differently today? Can you work out in a different way or change your eating habits or maybe start learning a new language? Sometimes making just one move *today* leads to making more, bolder moves tomorrow.

A bold move can be a life hack or tweak that helps you live better and more wisely, reducing waste, cutting costs, and using time more critically. Who doesn't want to live a more purposeful, intentional, thoughtful life? Or it could be a decision to reach out to someone you would like to know better—either someone you've never met or someone you haven't talked to in a long time. This could be an old friend, a past professor, a long-lost family member, or a colleague from an old job. It could be a friend of a friend, someone you see at the coffee shop every day, or someone you've heard of in your business. Why not take a risk and reach out, even if only on social media? The risk is relatively low. And who knows where that kind of networking might lead?

The bold moves I have been practicing recently all have to do with simplifying my life. The year 2020 certainly put some things in focus and had many people shifting priorities, including yours truly. Here are some adjustments I've been working on implementing in my life. Some are baby steps—others are bigger commitments—but I have been amazed at how this journey of change has invigorated me. Here are some bold simplifying ideas that might invigorate you as well:

- **Get real with material possessions and let go of what's not needed**—clothes, shoes, jewelry, makeup and grooming products, household décor (maybe even the house!). Go through your closet and look in the back of drawers and cabinets to see what you're really using. If you haven't worn or used something in a year, it's time to let it go. If it's not good quality, buh-bye. Try to rid yourself of an attachment to things. They don't make us happy. In fact, I've found it quite liberating to toss or give away what's not needed. When it comes to makeup, there are health and sanitary reasons as well as emotional ones. Liners and mascara shouldn't stay beyond six months. All makeup older than a year should go. You can extend eye shadow and blush by scraping off the top layer with a butter knife and spraying rubbing alcohol on top to disinfect.
- **Pare down schedules.** This is a big one, and it's one thing I believe 2020 actually helped us with. The pandemic shutdowns forced everything and everyone to slow down,

and this slowdown led many of us to rethink how we spend our time. This has been my biggest personal takeaway. I will never go back to a hectic, overbooked pace again or let other people determine what I do or don't do. That's not to say I won't have busy days. But I am determined to guard the pace of my life more carefully and dare to just say no to activities that don't fit my priorities or that I just don't wish to do.

- **Purchase with a purpose.** This means cutting back on random and impulsive buys. Everything new must fit a need. The new rule I'm following is that any new item I purchase means two items in my home must go. Not only has this helped me clear out my rooms and closets; it's helped me analyze whether I really need that new item.

- **Never pay full price for anything—and consider buying vintage!** To be honest, this isn't a new one for me. I have always been a "sale queen," and I love the hunt for a good deal. These days I'm also enjoying the hunt for gently used items, and I have found bargains in all sorts of places, from local resale stores to online high-end shops like the Real Real, Tradesy, Yoogi's Closet, and Poshmark. These are great places to score deals while helping someone else get rid of what's no longer serving them—or to hand off your own gently used items. One important note: my rule about getting rid of two items in my home when I bring in something new applies to sale and preowned items too!

- **Buy with a focus on quality.** All too often we just look for the number on a price tag and let that dictate whether we purchase something or not. But it's better to focus on whether that item will stand the test of time when it comes to longevity and style. Even if you have to spend a little more or buy fewer pieces, buying quality is ultimately more cost efficient. Wait and save for the good stuff or consider buying it secondhand. The quality pieces will be the last ones hanging in your closet after you've cleaned it out.

- **Rent if you can.** With companies like Rent the Runway and other retailers getting into the rental game, I will no longer spend hundreds on a gown for a gala or a dress for a wedding or special event. I also rented practically all my clothes for work except for a limited selection in my closet to buy time between rental arrivals. With rentals, you can mix it up every time and never wear the same thing twice.

- **Cut back on dry cleaning.** Because I rented more, my dry-cleaning bill went away, but I'm trying to lessen it even more. I've found that there are many natural spot cleaners for stains and laundry sprays to freshen up clothes (I like a lavender scent), so there's no real need to send everything to the cleaners anymore. Of course, it makes sense to buy fewer dry-clean-only items as well.

- **Use up products.** So many new things come on the market, from face creams to new foundations, I have often found myself with half-empty bottles after I've moved onto the next. These days, I'm trying not to fall victim to the latest ads or samples and to finish what I've purchased before moving on to the next new thing. I've learned that it will still be there in a month or six. And by then, something even more interesting might be available!

- **Do beauty at home.** Lately I've been experimenting with ways I can save money and simplify my life by reducing time in a salon or gym. For instance, I've found that while

I need a manicure every two weeks, my pedis with shellac can last a month if I make good use of a callus buffer and foot cream. I've also learned to touch up my own roots and do my own facials. And there are so many amazing self-tanning products now that you can do at home and that are much easier and more cost effective than going out for a spray tan. Some you can even mix in with your own moisturizers. I used to go for a spray tan every week and even had a spray tan membership that would automatically debit my payments from a card. Standing there cold and naked, with that awful-smelling spray covering me from head to toe—now that's something I really don't miss!

- **Break the gym habit.** It's so easy to step outside your front door for a walk or a jog. If you see a bench somewhere, you can stop and do some pushups or tricep dips on it. Lunge the last hundred yards back to your house. You'd be amazed what a great workout you can give yourself! There are also streaming exercise classes you can do in the comfort of your home—anything from yoga and Pilates to kickboxing and dance. This way you save on gym memberships and forgo the hassle of parking. If you love a yoga or exercise studio as I do, seek out opportunities to pay per class instead of shelling out for a monthly membership.

- **Order the right amounts.** I find that an appetizer plus an entrée is way too much food for me. I wind up taking half of it home, where it may or may not get eaten the next day. So now I order either one or the other. If an appetizer seems more appealing than the entrée, then I'll just order that!

- **Cancel online subscriptions and memberships.** It's amazing how quickly they add up, and if the fees are automatically deducted, it's easy to forget about them. I suggest going through your apps to see what you're paying for and how often you really use them. Do you have Pandora *and* Spotify? Do you need both? Also look into Netflix, Hulu, HBO Max, Showtime, Disney, and other streaming platforms. You'd be amazed at how the ten- or fifteen-dollar-a-month subscriptions can add up and be easily overlooked. It's worth your while to go through your bank and credit card statements to see what recurring monthly bills you have and whether they can be eliminated.
- **Look at your income and budget.** Decide how much you need to cover living expenses, pay off debt, make charitable contributions, and increase your savings. Then the rest is your play money. Make a financial plan and stick to it.

This list is not a prescription. I'm not writing to tell you what to do. These are just suggestions that I've used to show that even little changes can make a big difference in our lives. And every one of these requires the boldness to move ahead. We all could use a little kick start, and hopefully these provide some ideas.

Your Next Bold Move

The very word *bold* implies action. So now it's time to do just that—to act. Your next bold move can begin anywhere, at any time. And as we've seen, it can be large or small, a healthful new habit or a new life direction. Just let it begin.

A viewer from overseas shared how in her midthirties she felt it was time to pull the rug out from under a life that wasn't serving her. Not only did she make some big beauty changes, but she also changed cities and jobs—a complete life makeover! She's now in her forties, happy, and looking forward not just to what life brings but—as I often say—what she *chooses* for her life to bring. I'm always eager to share that it only gets better.

You've read from my YouTube viewers about some exciting bold moves they've made. So I ask you, what's *your* next step?

First, look over your vision boards and get reacquainted with yourself. What are your passions? What are your talents? It might help to consider the bold, risky moves you're made in your past that have paid off. Remembering them can give you a boost of self-esteem, courage, and pride that energizes your next move.

Then it might be good to get into your own head and ask yourself a series of thought-provoking questions about what your next moves could look like. Ask yourself,

- What are three things I have control over in my life right now?
- What is one change I could make in each of those areas?
- How would those changes impact my life?

I'm excited for you as you start this process. Hopefully one day I'll receive a letter from you about a new course you've set for yourself and how accomplished you feel as your life's chief navigator!

FOUR

·····················

THE UNEXPECTED
POWER OF REST

IMAGINE STANDING IN A SMALL room that's lined with multiple speakers and screens, each blasting a different song, podcast, video, news story, or movie all at once. It's loud in there, right? And distracting! You can hardly hear yourself think.

That's exactly how the world we live in can feel. Thanks to technology, we experience information overload almost constantly, from the moment we wake up until the moment our head hits the pillow—and often after that. If we aren't careful, we can short-circuit ourselves. I believe that today, more than ever, as we acknowledge just how entrenched we are in the information age, we must take purposeful steps to control that input and protect our minds and spirits. I think we need to turn down the volume on all that outside noise and listen more intently to that quiet voice inside.

So you're probably wondering—why a newscaster of

twenty-eight years and a YouTube content creator with nearly two million subscribers is advising you to be careful with your media consumption. Well, I'll tell you. It's really part and parcel to the overall message I yearn to share with women: you must create space in your life to discover—or *re*discover—who you really are. And I think a constant need for scrolling through our social-media feeds or binge-watching our favorite shows is merely a symptom of a problem many of us are facing: we have lost that connection with our passion and purpose. And if you linger too long in that land of internal disconnect, that place where you're focusing all your attention on other external forces or influences, you run the very real risk of flaming out. My goal is to help you rekindle that fire within and then keep it burning brightly.

To do all that's been laid out in the previous chapters, you must grant yourself the most precious and vital gift—and that is the gift of rest. Your gas tank is going to need to be topped off to successfully pull off any bold moves you're preparing to make— and rest is the only reliable way to fill it.

Rest is far more powerful than you may realize. It's so under-rated, and often ignored, but allowing your mind, body, and soul just to take a quiet breath and some time off can work wonders. Do you get enough? Think again. It's entirely possible that even when you think you're resting, you really aren't.

I should know. I fooled myself into believing I was getting plenty of "rest" for years, but my mind, if not my body, was con-stantly running. It took a lot of work to discover what rest really means for me, and I want to save you some time and help you get to your own place of rest much more quickly.

I'll never forget when the message of rest really hit home with me. It was a glorious September day in Houston, and I was on my way to a speaking engagement at Lakewood Church, which is pastored by Joel and Victoria Osteen. It was a women's conference called Love Your Life, and Victoria had invited me to do an interview touching on self-improvement, wellness, faith, family, organization, beauty, and style. That's a lot of topics, I know, but I cover them all on a weekly basis on my YouTube channel, so I felt confident about breaking them down into bite-size takeaways.

Thousands of women filled the seats of the sanctuary that day, and as Victoria conducted the interview, it was not lost on me what a privilege, honor, and true responsibility it was to be speaking in that setting. I always enjoy sharing my story and talking about how making bold moves has led to great blessings in my life. But when she was asking her final question, it occurred to me that this answer might be the one that resonated the most with the audience. It was to be the climax of the guidance I was there to offer that day.

Victoria asked, "What is the one thing you feel every woman should do to live her best life?"

Within milliseconds, something surreal happened. Three words came flooding into my mind, filling every space and leaving room for no other thought.

Quietly, and with deep empathy, I said, "Get your rest."

This hadn't been part of my plan that day. Rest wasn't on the docket. I was there to inspire, to motivate, to talk about how to live a passion-filled, purposeful life. Rest hadn't been part of that equation when I was scrawling out notes the night before. And yet when I said it, every eye was focused on me. More heads than I could count were nodding in intense agreement, and some women even started to applaud. I didn't quote Scripture, though many verses would've fit, but I believe with all my heart that God was there with me in that moment. I believe He wanted me to share with this group of women what had taken me fifty-two years to learn—that rest makes all the difference.

Why would those three little words have such an impact on a group of women of different backgrounds, ethnicities, ages, and stages? Simple. It's because most of us are so busy taking care of others that we have forgotten to care for ourselves. And in the process, we have actually lost the ability to care for others too!

The question of life balance often comes up on my YouTube channel. The comment section will overflow with women who say they feel lost, strung out, and unattractive. So many confess that they have become exhausted, agitated, estrogen-depleted creatures who do not measure up to their former selves—you know, those versions with good skin, fuller hair, great bods, and a skip in their step. They stopped prioritizing themselves long ago, and now they wonder who they are anymore.

And if I probe a little deeper, I learn that what they really are is *tired*. A lack of rest has far-reaching and deeply painful fallout. We must learn how to mitigate the negative effects of the "hurry up" attitude of today's world without rushing through life and missing what's really important.

I get it. There were days in my not-too-distant past when I could have checked some of those issues off my list. But not anymore. Having gone through a few rough patches and overextending, I have learned to come back to center. It was a conscious effort, steeped in mindfulness, prioritization, and prayer.

Crash Landings

My first lesson in sleep deprivation came in my early twenties, when I was working an overnight shift as a disc jockey at Mix 96.5. My job started at ten in the evening. I would take care of some audio production work, basically dubbing commercials from reel to reel to cart to be played on air. Then my on-air shift would begin at midnight and wrap up at five-thirty, when the morning show crew took over.

On most days I'd leave the studio, have breakfast, and then go home to go to bed. But I was also signed up with two modeling and talent agencies to generate extra work and income, which meant I sometimes had auditions for commercial or print work or, if I was lucky, some actual jobs. My sleep was sporadic at best, mostly during the day. My life revolved around work and nothing else.

One morning after finishing my DJ shift, I went home and grabbed a two-hour nap before heading out for a nine o'clock audition. Getting up from that brief rest was painful, but what was even more painful was driving into a large white van right next to me on the road where I needed to make a right turn. How do you not see a large white van? I wasn't even aware it was there until I heard a loud crash and realized I had ruined the right front end of my car.

I initially thought the only damage was to my vehicle, but then the epiphany came that my health, both mental and physical, was suffering. I came close to quitting my job because I simply couldn't take the crazy hours, low pay, and side hustle much longer.

I confided as much to our morning-show DJ, who was a friend. Apparently he knew I was going to be promoted to the late-night shift from the overnight one, so he coaxed me into sticking it out a little while longer. He didn't actually mention the promotion, but he did promise that I would be rewarded for my efforts and work ethic. He just "knew" it.

I held out hope that he was right and stuck it out. Thankfully, not long after that fateful conversation, I did receive the promotion. That meant I could go to sleep at two in the morning instead of six and develop a slightly more normal sleep routine. I also got to keep a job and stay with a company that was nurturing me and providing an amazing training ground for the fulfilling career that lay ahead—a career that would come with sleep issues of its own.

Getting Serious About No

To understand how rest fits into the rest of our lives, let's consider what happens when we lift weights to build muscle. When we stress the muscles, we actually create tiny tears in the muscle fibers, which in turn cause soreness. That ache is the body's way of saying, "Ease up and let those tears heal so the muscle can grow." Effective weight training is thus a delicate balance of lifting and laying off. If you just keep pushing and pulling, day in and day out, you risk injury, and you won't get the results you want.

The same thing happens in our mental, emotional, and spiritual lives. We aren't meant to expend constant effort. Without a balance of exertion and rest, we simply cannot grow—and we also risk creating real damage to our bodies, our minds, and our spirits. And although sleep is important, it's not the only kind of rest we need. We also desperately need mental, emotional, and spiritual downtime—time for ourselves, time to think and dream and just chill out. And to get that necessary time-out in our day-to-day lives, we need to set boundaries. If we don't make time for rest, no one will do it for us, and our lives will suffer as a result.

I believe that women connect with my story and my content because they need to know it is okay to invest in who they are or what they want to be. But they also need to hear that it is okay to say no, to cultivate the time to develop themselves, read, meditate, pray, or simply rest. Setting that kind of boundary is a significant piece of the puzzle when it comes to investing in ourselves. But it's also one of the hardest things for most women to do. We often pay lip service to "the power of no," but most of us find it incredibly difficult to put into practice.

I was the worst at it, a consummate people-pleaser. The word *yes* seemed to flow out of my mouth before I could even catch it. Then came the *Why did I do that?* self-talk. Frustrated with my loaded calendar and my inability to sit still long enough for a proper exhale, I was beginning to feel shock waves through my body. The consequence of not honoring my own needs came in the form of moodiness, depression, and anxiety, all of which had once been foreign to me. I found myself angry at my lack of self-control and self-preservation. *Why are everyone else's needs more important than my own? How am I going to be good at anything when I'm trying to be there for everything?*

My professional schedule didn't help, of course. Career-wise, I've worked every shift in the book—late nights, mornings, afternoons, and finally late evenings. Each required a different sleep schedule, and transitioning from one to another was hard on my system. Factor in children, marriage, YouTube, social media, community commitments, family, friends, and aging parents, and eventually I reached the point that I was about ready to fall apart (and I did).

People kept asking me, "How do you do it all?" I would smile and nod and say, "I just try not to think about it." But something needed to give before I found myself colliding into another white van.

So, I decided to get serious about learning to say no. In some ways it was the boldest move I had ever made in my life! I decided I would no longer commit to every charity event that came my way, every dinner or lunch invitation, every favor asked, simply because I felt I'd be missing out or hurting someone's feelings.

It took a while for me to get in the swing of my new commitment. My noes were apologetic at first, softened with hints that maybe next time or next week I might say yes. I would leave the door slightly open, knowing full well that wasn't my real intention. Guilt! Guilt! Guilt! But as time went by and I continued to practice my gracious noes, the guilt subsided. I became honest with my responses—grateful and appreciative for an invitation, but true to myself about my fatigue or my attention to a project (such as this book) or just my need to sit still after a hectic news week.

Do you know what happened? People understood. The responses were, "Boy, I feel you! I wish I weren't so busy. I'd give anything to do nothing today."

What does that tell me? Everything.

So how about you? Run a brain scan over your life; I'm sure it looks a bit different today than it did a few years ago.

The COVID Pause

I think it's safe to say that how we all operate has shifted dramatically since the discovery of the SARS-CoV-2 virus in late 2019. The resulting COVID-19 pandemic essentially defined our lives in 2020 and continued into 2021. I suspect that we'll still be feeling the effects by the time you read this book.

For many, living with COVID meant staying at home—juggling work, home, and children's education while conducting outside contact through the Zoom platform on phones and computers. You may have officed out of the living room with your husband next door in the kitchen, assuming you both got to keep your jobs. Factor in mask mandates, health concerns, and other issues, and our lives took on whole different levels of stress, uncertainty, vulnerability, and exhaustion, while the only entertainment available was binge-watching favorite TV series until the wee hours of the morning. We all love our families, but keep everyone under the same roof for days, weeks, and months on end—well, you would have to be a saint to happily sail through that scenario! The winners in the entire situation were family pets, who got more of us than they ever imagined they would.

I thank my lucky stars that I had a job where I could physically show up and interact with my colleagues. I know that was a huge part of my being able to keep my sanity in this new "not so normal" normal. How ironic. I was overconnected and overstimulated before, and then I was grateful for any connection I could possibly get.

What does that tell us? Balance is key, and how we find that balance in our lives is as unique as we are.

For me, the blessing in all of this is that the outside forces

I was battling—the overcommitting and overextending—simply stopped because things just weren't happening. Life shut down in 2020. Things closed. I had my work at Channel 2, my YouTube content to produce, and my family to care for, and the rest was pretty chill. There were days when I actually got bored! Say what? I wasn't used to that one. The uncontrollable events in life slowed my pace and helped bring me back to what matters. No matter how things change in the future in terms of what can't be controlled, I know what I need and what I don't need. I've felt both and will be a better steward of coming back to center.

As your mind goes through the hours in your day and how they're filled, where are your opportunities to unplug? If you have children, I know their needs are probably your first priority. Factor in a career, tending to a house, a spouse, aging parents perhaps, and suddenly the hours have dwindled to minutes when it comes to time for yourself. You must be tired. You have every right to be. But for your own health, wellness, and sanity, not to mention your ability to achieve some lofty goals you're setting for yourself, I really want you to focus on getting good and consistent rest. Not every day will be a win, but setting your intention will send you well on your way.

I want to address rest in two stages. One is sleep, and the other is seeking moments during the day to unwind.

The Sleep Solution

Do you get enough sleep? If you're like many Americans, the answer may be no. According to a 2016 study by the Centers for

Disease Control and Prevention, one in three Americans is not getting enough sleep or enough quality sleep on a regular basis.[1] And the consequences of chronic sleep deprivation can be serious. According to an NPR report, "Sleepless individuals are more prone to obesity, heart disease, stroke and diabetes, as well as mental health problems such as anxiety, unstable moods, and even thoughts of suicide."[2]

The reasons for this are not surprising. People's lives are overstuffed with work and other commitments. Stress keeps many of us wide-eyed at night. Technology keeps us caught up in an "always on" cycle. And any number of physical issues, from chronic pain to sleep apnea, can keep our systems revving when all we want to do is sleep.[3]

Ask any menopausal woman about this issue, for instance, and she'll probably look at you with a furrowed brow, give you the stink eye, and unleash her sarcastic tongue about her lack of satisfaction. Retorts like, "Let's see, I toss and turn all night from night sweats—covers on, covers off, hot, cold, hot, cold—then I have to pee. I get up, and then my brain won't shut down, and I'm thinking about what I have to do the next day, and then what do you know? It *is* the next day!"

Boy, can I relate.

It was around this point in my life that I sought bioidentical hormone replacement therapy, then purchased both a big bottle of melatonin and a fitness watch. I know, one of these things is not like the other. But the feature of that timekeeper that drew me in was the sleep tracking it offered. The step count was meh in my eyes. I was enthralled and somewhat paranoid knowing this device was going to let me know not only how long (or short) I slept, but would also track my REM, deep sleep, and awake stages. It would compile this information and give me an actual sleep score. My sleep was being graded!

The next night, the fully charged band on my left wrist and eager to see what my new sleep researcher would say about my slumber, I climbed into bed. Lights out.

The minute I awoke, I wiped my foggy eyes, stretched my arms to find my readers on the nightstand, and opened the phone app at warp speed to check my chart. Did it reflect how I felt, which seemed pretty good at the moment, though still in a foggy haze? Sure enough, it was pretty dang close. Colorful lines arched and danced across my phone. Deep here, light there, awake over here. I studied the graph over and over. Then came the score, a number with a little circle around it, just in case I had any trouble finding it amid all those readouts.

I got a 90—a heck of a score for a first night!

I've had the watch for a while now, and my scores aren't terrible. Granted, I've never reached a perfect 100. I think you'd have to be in a coma to get one of those. But my scores range from 70 to 90 max. Don't ask me about days when I score under 70. I'm not writing or producing content on those days; I'm probably hiding in my room so I don't bite someone's head off. Thankfully, those days are few and far between.

I am no sleep expert, but as someone who adores sleep and will do anything to secure a nine-hour night, I do have my strategies. They are simple rules that if put into play can help almost anyone get closer to their sleep goal, no matter what that may be.

- **Keep a consistent sleep schedule.** Our bodies want to settle into a rhythm and depend on it. If we listen closely, they'll tell us when they're tired. But all too often we push past those natural cues. We tell ourselves, *One more episode. One more scroll through social media. One more email.* Before we know it we're wired and not tired, so we carry on. Sound familiar? That's why you need to actually schedule your sleep time, at least at first. If you have to, set a reminder in your calendar that it's time to sleep, just like you'd set one for a business meeting. Make your sleep time important enough to write down. And make sure you're building in enough time to wind down first so that you can secure enough hours to feel and function at your absolute best.

- **Pay attention to your sleep environment.** Try to eliminate noise and distraction. A blaring television, blue light from devices, people talking outside your bedroom or in earshot are big no-no's in my book. Our brains need the right environment to unwind and to prepare for a gentle drift into sleep. I personally love a dark room and absolute quiet. I'm the one who puts tape or a sock in front of any light that comes from a TV, clock, phone, you name it. I even turn remotes upside down. For me, the room I sleep in has to be pitch-black to the point where, if I have to get up to go to the bathroom, I might break a toe on something. That's a sacrifice I'm willing to make!

- **Check the room temperature.** Research shows that colder rooms lead to a better night's sleep. According to Sleep.org, the ideal room temperature should be between sixty and seventy degrees Fahrenheit. A cold room also helps with the production of melatonin, the hormone that can trigger sleepiness. And as a bonus, according to research by the National Institute of Health, sleeping in a cold room can help your body burn fat![4] That certainly helps us menopausal gals. Besides, why did we buy all those layers of bedding in the first place? For the dog?

- **Develop some bedtime rituals.** Once you have the conditions right, your brain may still need a little coaxing. I love to read at night before bed with a little book light. I get to feed my brain with something of interest, and it's a wonderful way to give it a healthy sense of fatigue to the point that it wants to shut off. Also, I have discovered two phone apps that helped me wind down and reconnect with my breath. One is called Calm and the other Pray. (Both are available for either iPhone or Android.) These are beautiful ways to meditate your way into a slumber, either hearing God's Word or learning how to connect and focus on your breathing so you gain control over how your body relaxes and can learn to cue it at any time.
- **Consider earplugs.** I have learned that any little noise can trigger my eyes to open. I find that sleeping with earplugs safely keeps me in silence, and they can even diminish any loud vibrations from your partner, if you know what I'm saying. If you're a light sleeper, earplugs can be a lifesaver.

Your winning formula for restful bliss will set the stage for you to tackle the world in any way you need or desire. A good night's sleep allows you to wipe the chalkboard of your previous day perfectly clean, no chicken scratches or faded white streaks remaining—the perfect surface to scribble away on. You may have a lot going on in the world that you're designing (or redesigning) for yourself—work, family, hobbies, self-care, self-exploration, new approaches to old problems, and so on. Starting new each morning will help you tackle all those pursuits with fresh enthusiasm. It will also help you recognize and experience God's glory in your life—it's hard to see things clearly when you're tired and worn.

By all means, seek medical help if your sleep problems continue. Remember that you are your most valuable investment. You *deserve* to get the problem addressed by a medical professional.

For instance, I've been on bioidentical hormone replacement therapy for years now to address menopausal symptoms, including sleep disruption, but it's not an exact science. One formula doesn't fit all, and our bodies and hormone levels change constantly. Finding an open-minded health and wellness specialist who is willing to listen, work with you, and adjust dosages until you feel right is critical.

For women who can't be on hormone replacement therapy, there are other, natural sleep assists available, from melatonin to 5-HTP to magnesium, valerian root, lavender, and glycine.[5] There's no reason to sit around and suffer, and there are too many good practitioners available, so don't settle if you feel you're not getting help. Your wellness begins with proper sleep, and I hope you covet it!

Rest Snacks

So now let's talk about unwinding during the day. Rewriting your life's script takes effort in the midst of life's duties and obligations. It's easy to succumb to burnout. Starting your day off on the right track is one thing, but staying on track is another. That's where I like to create what I call rest "snackables"—bite-size moments of rest for both mind and body. Just fifteen minutes of respite can be enough to keep you going throughout the day. Here are just a few ideas for enjoying a rest snack in the midst of your busy life:

- **Meditate.** As I mentioned, I listen to the Calm app at night, but I use it at other times too. The app guides me through the most wonderful ten minutes of deep breathing, quieting the noise in my head (without punishing myself if it's a struggle at times) and then listening to a delightful and inspiring message I can ponder as the hours creep by. Deep breaths with counted inhales and exhales are so good for oxygenating the body and calming the mind. When you start practicing moments like these, you begin to realize what shallow breathers we are when we're not practicing it. I find those ten little minutes in a corner of a quiet room work like a magical reset button in my brain. I walk out in a peaceful state of mind, ready for what's to come.

- **Take a moment with God's Word.** If my brain is stressed and overwhelmed from work, children, or anything that's taxing me, I often find respite in reading a short passage of Scripture. There are so many verses that focus on gratitude, strength, wisdom, and fighting the weariness. It helps to prepare a list of these as a resource—maybe on your phone or an index card—but even a quick Google search can help you find a passage with the right message for what you're needing at the moment. What a great way to shift to a place of gratitude and an *I shall overcome* mindset.

- **Stretch.** Most of us these days feel the ache and strain in our neck and shoulders from too much sitting and too much time looking down at devices, and the resulting "text neck" can really do a number on us.[6] Taking a quick moment to release the tension is a great acknowledgment that our bodies need a break too. I'll roll my head around the front, back, and from side to side to loosen up my neck. Shoulder rolls help, and so does stretching my arms way up high and then interlacing them behind my back. Then, if I have a few minutes more, I can get even more benefit from stretching my whole body.

- **Get out and move.** As you may have seen on my social media posts, I'm a big fan of taking a walk, preferably outside. One thing the COVID pandemic did was get people outdoors again. Bike sales went through the roof, and I saw many families pedaling together along neighborhood streets like ducks on a lake. It was a joyful sight to see so many people outside getting exercise and spending time together as a family. Lucky for me, I live in Houston, where the weather is favorable for outdoor activities year-round (except for maybe July and August). My walks during this time became my private escape to listen to my favorite Spotify playlist with a crazy array of disco, pop, bossa nova, classic rock, rockin' country, and great '80s tunes. That music and movement also provided me the opportunity to inhale what I was grateful for in the moment and exhale all the rest. I would come back home after my three miles feeling a blend of invigoration and peace, not to mention the mind-healing effects of just being out in nature. Even a shorter walk around the block could be enough to get my blood moving and refresh my mind.
- **Connect with nature.** Walking isn't the only way to enjoy the benefits of being in the natural world. You can

also grab a yoga mat and head outside to stretch and move in the sunshine or the breeze. Or if you can't get out and you've been sitting at your computer for too long, at least take a moment to shift your eyes toward a window. See what kinds of birds are in view. What are the squirrels doing? Are the leaves blowing? The clouds shifting? Sometimes just gazing at the beauty and simplicity outside is enough to bring calmness to our minds.

- **Don't forget the power of smell.** I have one of those aromatherapy diffusers I like to keep near me. Drop in some lavender essential oil—or tea tree or lemon or orange, whatever floats your boat. Each inhale will bring more sensory joy. (If you have pets, do some research beforehand; some essential oils are toxic for them.) My favorite escape is combining aromatherapy with a hot bath—talk about a mental and physical softening. This is actually a great thing to do before bed. The state of relaxation it induces makes it easy to slide under the covers for lights-out.

These rest snackables during the day are a perfect accompaniment to your efforts for a deeper and more refreshing night's sleep. Think of them as opportunities to recharge your mind and body so you can approach your life, your goals, and those you love from a place of peace and contentment. They will help you accomplish all that you've set out for yourself.

Pacing is everything, and you are important enough to grant yourself a break when needed. I'd rather seek forgiveness than ask for permission in this area! Listen to your amazing body. It tells you exactly what it needs.

If Rest Eludes You, Dig a Little Deeper

If you find that you've been resisting rest, there may be something deeper going on. Some people are driven to keep going and never stop, operating at such a frantic pace that they barely have time to think. It's possible that such busyness is a strategy to *not* think. Sometimes, if we are unhappy or unfulfilled in certain aspects of our lives, we will pack our schedules to oblivion with the intent of not allowing one brain cell to sway from its duty and risk deep thought. Too much empty space in the calendar could give the mind the opportunity to wander, and then what? We might have to acknowledge that we're not too happy with this existence we've created, the work we're doing, the people we're with. The problem with such avoidance tactics is that they only work for so long before something breaks down—our bodies, our spirits, our relationships. In the meantime, they keep us moving through life machinelike, without deep connection to ourselves and others.

Learning to rest means we're willing to let go and swim to our ocean depths, where it's dark and quiet and only we can hear. It's our space to fortify and receive, anytime and anyplace. Rest is our private sanctuary, doors wide open, allowing us to unapologetically seal our eyes tightly shut and truly see within.

FIVE

FEAR, FAITH, AND FUHGEDDABOUDIT

A VERSE FROM THE BOOK OF Isaiah holds a powerful re-assurance that we are not alone on this earth and that most fear has no place in our hearts and minds:

> So do not fear, for I am with you;
>   do not be dismayed, for I am your God.
> I will strengthen you and help you;
>   I will uphold you with my righteous right
>   hand. (41:10)

That's a powerful command: "Do not fear." But is that even possible—or desirable? The answer is absolutely—with one caveat.

Not all fear is created equal, you see. There are some cases where fear is necessary. Fear can actually be a gift; it can help us survive. If you're attacked by a bear in the woods, I most certainly wouldn't expect you to have a calm and confident demeanor while you're exploring rapid-fire survival strategies to secure your spot in the gene pool. No, you would be terrified. And part of your terror would involve what is called the fight-or-flight instinct. Your breathing would instantly increase and your heart rate would speed up, fueling your muscles so you could react appropriately. We've all seen or heard stories of people who displayed incredible, almost superhuman strength to escape a life-or-death situation.

Such fear is a natural and helpful response to a real threat, and we would be foolish to ignore it or try to overcome it. But what if fear is an overreaction to something we've imagined, more of an irrational response based on what-ifs running through the mind? Or what if the fear is triggered by the memory of something that happened in the past or worry of what might happen in the future, not something that threatens us in the present? And what if those feelings of fear make us stop and keep us from moving forward? Fear of change, fear of the unknown, fear of failure, fear of what others might think, fear of what *you* might think—any of these can sabotage our well-laid plans for resetting our lives. Suddenly there we are, paralyzed in a mind and body that was designed to act.

This type of fear is what I call imagined fear. Actually, that term is a little misleading; the fear itself is real—you feel it and respond to it. The "imagined" part has to do with the threat that inspires the fear. We may conjure unnecessary visions of danger when none are present. Or we may imagine that a real threat is bigger or more dangerous than it really is and assume it can't be overcome. That's what stops us in our tracks and sabotages our best efforts to change and grow.

I've known that kind of sabotaging fear. We all have. But we all have the perfect weapon available to us to fight our imagined fears. That weapon is faith.

Faith in ourselves.

And especially faith in our heavenly Father.

The Power of Faith

In my late thirties, when I was married to my first husband, we struggled with fertility issues. I know countless couples can relate to this. It was gut-wrenching because we believed with every fiber of our being that we were meant to be parents. It was an emotionally charged experience, to say the least. Ultimately we made the decision to go through in vitro fertilization (IVF).

I remember those days of hormone injections and egg collection—I felt like a walking henhouse. The doctors fertilized eight of my eggs, four of which appeared to be viable, but in the end, only one was ready for implanting. Because the likelihood of becoming pregnant through IVF is very low, the doctors prefer to implant more than one embryo. They were not optimistic about our odds if they implanted just one. In fact, they said we had about a 1 percent chance of getting pregnant with that single embryo. They encouraged us to freeze it and go through the process again to create more embryos. But I was physically and emotionally depleted by that time. We decided to roll the dice.

So there I was lying on the table after the procedure, slightly inverted (to increase the odds) and pretty emotional, ranging from tears to laughter, with a strong urge to pee. Then, out of nowhere, I had this overwhelming desire to pray. I had been raised in an agnostic home, and as loving, thoughtful, and purpose-driven as my upbringing was, prayer was not a part of it. I had zero experience with talking to God at that point in my life, so you can see why this urge felt foreign to me.

But I did it. I prayed—big and bold. It felt strange and unfamiliar, yet so right.

Days passed, and I wondered if the exercise—the IVF and the praying—had been in vain. I even had a little scare days later, making me really question that impulse of mine.

Then, lo and behold, I got pregnant with my son! And a little nugget of faith was planted in me as well.

But my faith journey after that was not zero to sixty in a matter of seconds. Not at all. It was a slow burn for years. I continued to pray during my pregnancy, thanking God for the gift of carrying this child and praying for a healthy baby boy. Those prayers were infrequent and felt like they came more from a place of begging than receiving. Still, they were a clear acknowledgment of what I was coming to believe—that there was something bigger and greater than me at work in this situation.

I hadn't really learned how to pray just yet, and I hadn't attended a church. But I was about to get some great inspiration on going before God with boldness and expectation.

My son, Styles, was born, and it was the most precious day. I'll never forget feeling that newborn skin up against mine and seeing his puffy lips (runs in the family) and sweet eyes. But once we brought him home, the struggles began. As you've read, his first year in this world was a challenge for us all. Several years later my marriage disintegrated. And it was in January 2010, during my divorce, that faith really came into play for me.

I knew deep down that I couldn't do this alone. It was too

hard being the single, working mother of a child with health challenges and then facing emotional challenges from going through a divorce on top of that. That's when I started attending Lakewood Church, and I dedicated my life to God.

I've done life without Him, and I've done it with Him.

I know which I prefer.

For me, faith is the answer to so many, if not all, of life's questions and challenges, and I can tell you from experience that it is the greatest weapon ever formed against fear.

Whether we are consciously aware of it or not, fear dictates many of the decisions we make. It is often the primary driver of the decision to stay exactly, precisely where we are rather than choosing to change and grow. That's why I want you to abandon fear. I mean it. I want you to leave it on the side of the road and not give it a second glance in your rearview mirror. Abandoning fear enables you to be bold and to take risks. It frees you to move forward in your life. But the only way you'll be able to do this is to choose a new modus operandi.

Faith.

Before I knew God, I would've looked at moments in my life when I was somehow protected from a bad occurrence or when an incredible opportunity came about and attributed those moments to my own willpower or sheer luck. But now, looking back on those moments, I see that God was present. I can see the special ways in which He showed up in my life. And because of this understanding, moving forward, I know I can rely on my faith to overpower any fear that might rise up.

We've all experienced hardships, and we likely will again. They will come in varying intensities and at different times in our lives. I've learned not to try to pray them away, because that's futile. But I've also learned that I cannot live in fear of the next "bad" thing that might happen. Instead, I pray for strength, wisdom, and guidance to get through whatever is happening to me. There's growing in the suffering, and while the waters may be murky at the moment, clarity happens later when God's purpose is revealed.

I've also learned that *how* I pray is just as important as the prayer itself. There's a difference between "God, please help me not fall during tomorrow's rock climb. I'm really nervous and don't want to hurt myself. My family couldn't get by without me" versus "Heavenly Father, thank You for equipping me with all I need to tackle that big rock tomorrow. It may be high, but You are higher, and through You all things are possible. I know You will cover me with protection and allow the thrilling feeling of taking on something new and challenging to overflow and provide a sense of accomplishment. Amen!"

My pastor has taught me to pray bold prayers like that, with expectancy. To approach my heavenly Father, who loves me, with words that honor what He is capable of, which is everything. I do my part, and I pray *knowing* that He does His.

There's a difference between asking and knowing. Asking for help is one thing. Knowing we will be helped is another. The beauty is for us to keep our spirit eyes wide open to see how that will work itself out. It may not happen in a way we expect, but it will happen in God's way and His timing. I've learned to be understanding and patient with that reality, for therein lies the peace that comes from prayer and faith.

Any bold move in my life now starts with a conversation with my God. He is my counselor, confidant, and most gracious listener. I put it out to Him, and then I put the rest on me. Faith isn't about sitting back and waiting for God to work behind the scenes. Faith is about making your chess moves. Honor the queen within, guard her well, and then use her abilities to strike at the most opportune moments. You'll see the blessings pour in!

Building the Faith to Conquer Fear

God gifted each of us with a most magnificent brain of unimaginable capabilities. I'm sure we only scratch at the surface of what it can do, though we can always dig deeper. Fear, on the other hand, is a nasty itch, and while we scratch to alleviate the irritating sensation, we must also learn to diminish its presence so we don't end up marked and wounded.

The best way to do this, in my opinion, is to tackle the little fears so you can build up the self-esteem and courage to go after the bigger ones.

The best way is to *act now!*

You may be thinking, *Where do I start? This sounds exciting! I can conquer that paralyzing monster once and for all!* You can most certainly bring it down to size, look it in the eyes, and say, "Every step I take in conquering you makes you smaller, less frightening, and less significant in my life." Just that acknowledgment is freeing. Saying it out loud—maybe even shouting it forcefully—is even more freeing! Proclaim that you are leading the way. You're on this planet to live out your glory, not to sit on the sidelines wishing for something better, envious of what others may have and feeling like you got dealt a bad hand of cards. I hope you can believe in something more and act deservingly.

Conquering the little fears helps you conjure the courage to go after the big ones. If you've already made some bold moves and invested in yourself based on what you've read so far, then it's likely you've already begun tackling the fear of change. You've tried a new hairstyle or makeup look and switched out some things in your wardrobe. Maybe your new look was a great success and you realized you had nothing to be afraid of in the first place. Or maybe you've experienced a failure or two and discovered the drop wasn't as bad as you had imagined. And even if it was bad, hopefully you learned something about resilience and playing to your other strengths. In all of that you've been practicing how to handle fear with faith.

My walk in this arena started with that first Sun In experiment in middle school and continues to this day. My TV and YouTube viewers have seen transformation after transformation, usually at six-month intervals. I'm not sure why that is, but a look back at earlier posts and broadcasts shows it clearly. My TV station's general manager always said to viewers who would call or write in about my hair, "Don't worry if you don't like it. It'll be different in six months."

I can only imagine the number of hair-raising comments he had received! But for every ten or twenty that might have come his way, for me it's a daily assault. The double-edged sword is that I love to show women the power of change, to loosen the grip of fear and encourage them to go for it. But on the other hand, I must deal with the criticism and judgment from those who don't like what I'm doing.

Change is scary to people, even a new hairstyle on a newscaster or YouTuber. Some see me a certain way, and if I depart from what they prefer, they seem to take offense. Some will even take sides; I have my auburn camps, my dark brown camps, and my blonde camps. No matter what shade I'm sporting, I'm going to hear from at least two of them about how it's not their favorite: "too harsh" or "too light; it washes you out," "too long," "too short," and on and on and on.

Fear and Fuhgeddaboudit

I have been subjected to judgment my entire career, but the advent of social media has really escalated it. I've had to overcome the fear of what I call keyboard courage—people's willingness to share unsolicited comments and opinions without regard for the impact on the other person's feelings. Nowadays it can be done anonymously, so in some cases I don't even have the opportunity to reply.

When you're on the receiving end of such a barrage, it can sometimes get into your head, leaving you resentful. I've certainly had my moments in the past when it got under my skin. But I've been able to work through those moments by unleashing another fear-fighting tool.

I just fuhgeddaboudit.

That's right. I've learned that some battles simply aren't worth fighting. Sometimes it works best just to ignore a threat and let it roll off your back. Armed with faith in God and in yourself, you can just forget about it.

I found this strategy is especially effective when it comes to those unsolicited judgments. I'm always astonished as to how readily people offer opinions about someone other than themselves. Some don't mean any harm. They really seem to think they're helping, as if their assessment will finally get the other person to see things straight. What's lacking, however, is the empathy or foresight to understand that their judgments might be hurtful. Others use judgment deliberately to inflict pain. In either case, instead of shining the light inward to reflect and heal, they cast a blinding laser beam outward that has the capacity to sear and do serious harm.

If we let it, that is.

But we don't have to let it.

We must be careful guardians against this kind of assault, putting up a shield that keeps the beam from penetrating and generating fear. That shield involves both your faith in your God and your faith in *you*—that you are worthy, capable, and have every right to pursue whatever changes in your life you're seeking. That's what makes it possible to ignore the naysayers. Faith makes fuhgeddaboudit possible.

I've found it also helps to shift my thinking about the possible origin of these types of comments. Understanding the psychology behind people's fear of change and their willingness to judge and condemn makes it easier to ignore their painful judgments.

Many people come from a negative upbringing, where words of condemnation were spoken over them instead of words of empowerment. Some may feel like failures after a series of bad choices or unworthy of redemption and blessing. Insecurity, anxiety, or difficult social and emotional predispositions could lead them to feel isolated or powerless. No two are alike, but negativity almost always stems from a place of hurt and pain. At least I choose to see it that way—to simply feel bad for the author of the note or the speaker of the words and not take their judgment personally.

There is an incredible freedom that arises when we stop

basing our sense of self-worth on what others think of us and release ourselves from their judgment. You can't please everyone, so why even try?

There's a lot of power in fuhgeddaboudit.

The Driver's Seat

Here's another way to look at imagined fear. Have you ever noticed that when you're a passenger in a car, miles can go by where you don't take in much of your surroundings? Land, streets, and structures just streak by in a kind of blur. But when you're in the driver's seat, your senses come alive. Your vision is sharp. Your eyes dart about, taking in what's in front, to the side, and behind. You grip the steering wheel tightly or loosely, depending on road conditions. You're aware of the controls on the dash—speed, gas level, and other information that can determine the success of the trip. The temperature in the vehicle is set for optimum comfort. The sunroof is open or closed to either allow the subtle warmth of daylight on your shoulders or block the sun's intense rays.

This heightened sense of existing only comes from being in the driver's seat in our lives, where there's risk and reward. Paralyzing fear might prevent you from driving that car, afraid someone might hit you. Faith in the fact that you're an experienced driver gets you excited to get behind the wheel, looking forward to where that trip will take you, knowing the risks full well, simply from a statistical perspective but not an emotional one.

That's an effective compartmentalizing of fear. There's a rational awareness that yes, something could go wrong, but in all likelihood it won't because you're not reckless behind the wheel and you trust your skill set to get you where you need to go. You have faith in your abilities, and before your excursion you might give a shout-out to God and thank Him in advance for your safe and pleasurable road trip.

That's the kind of activated faith that rises up, pleases God, and makes imagined fear look like a useless troll, smaller in stature and limited in power.

If you're like me and prefer being in the driver's seat, there are some simple starts to help you tackle fear in a steady, progressive way. What I love about the "beauty from the outside in" approach is that the baby steps used in conquering fear over our appearance lead to the courage to take bigger steps in deeper areas of our lives. I want you to rise up in your faith to give it a go!

I'm hoping you've already experienced abandoning imagined fear when it comes to changing your hair, knowing that it will grow back. Changing your hair is low risk. The same goes for makeup. If you don't like a new look, you can wipe it off. After taking smaller risks like these, you can begin to take bigger, deeper risks in your life and enjoy bigger rewards. There are many places to start to help you gain confidence in this endeavor. The more you practice, the braver you'll be!

Nine Imagined Fears to Fight or Fuhgeddabout

One of my favorite videos I ever published is called "Top 10 Things I Don't Worry About over 50." In the video I explored some of the points I saw as advantages that came from getting older. Looking back at it now, I see that the "worries" I pointed out also involve imagined fears that people at any age can—and should—fight and get past. So I've edited and adapted the list to focus more specifically on fear.

You may see yourself in these scenarios. I've certainly been there, although I've finally been able to put most of them behind me. The truth is, many of us waste too much time fretting about these common issues, no matter what our age or stage of life. If we can summon the faith to fight them, fuhgeddabout them, or both, we will all be better off.

As you work through this list, keep in mind that it may be aspirational for you, not something you can check off quickly. "Don't fear" is something we all need to grow into, not (usually) something we achieve in an instant. Some items will seem easier than others, depending on your background, your personality, and so many other circumstances. But I'm here to tell you that these common fears don't need to paralyze you or sabotage your life. With faith and fuhgeddaboudit, you can leave them behind you.

Fear Issue #1: What Other People Think

It is so freeing to give up people-pleasing—which is really a form of fear. If you put too much value on what others think and getting their approval, you will fall short every time because you simply cannot please everyone. Wear your hair the way your husband likes it, then suddenly your mother says the style isn't age appropriate. Get a pixie cut after your girlfriend's input, then suddenly your husband is furrowing his brow. You can't win! When your every choice is based on another's wish, you'll find yourself drifting farther and farther from your authentic self.

Does that mean you shouldn't be thoughtful or try to bring pleasure to those you care about? Of course not. Does it mean you shouldn't take other people's feelings and opinions into consideration? Again, no. But if you find that a fear of what others might think is overriding your own good judgment, undermining your self-worth, or preventing you from doing something you really want to do, then it's time to pay attention.

Overcoming fear in this area means you stop sizing up your self-worth according to what others think and stop letting their opinions determine the choices you make. When you realize that not everyone will be pleased with everything you do, then you can set yourself free to please yourself.

To be honest, I have never been that much of a people-pleaser. I've always marched to the beat of my own drum, and early in life I made the choice to do that in the public eye, knowing what scrutiny may follow. I definitely wasn't going to abandon my authentic self in the name of caution. *No bueno!* But I did struggle initially with the criticism that seemed to be coming at me. I could have played it safe to avoid it, going against my own undercurrent. Learning to ignore the judgments that sometimes pile up on me has been a process, and I like to resort to a little bit of humor to get me through.

Today, if someone offers me an unsolicited opinion, I will graciously say, "You're most certainly entitled to your opinion. I've learned long ago that you can't please everyone all the time. It's like the old joke 'He who runs after car gets exhausted.' It's tiring enough just trying to please myself! I'm sure you understand, and thank you for taking the time to write." Not long after I hit Send, I usually get the response, "Oh, well, I hope I didn't offend you! I just love the way you aren't afraid to do things. I guess I just preferred such-and-such, but you just keep being you! I love your content!"

We Texans like to kill 'em with kindness.

If a person in your life makes you feel less loved or less valuable because of a new hairstyle—or any other change—then consider the next thing that might need to get trimmed is that person. True colors (no pun intended) can quickly be revealed in a situation like that. Could it be that your own fear of change is tied to what you might suspect about someone in your life? This can certainly prompt some important conversations about value, acceptance, and making someone feel special no matter what.

Fear Issue #2: Food and Body Image

Our society has really done a number on us women. The biggest fear for many of us is not living up to an idealized concept of beauty. And who can blame us? Images of female perfection—some natural, some photoshopped, some completely computer generated—flood our pages and our screens. Social media feeds highlight all the right angles and use all the right filters. It's hard to miss the message that we have to look a certain way to be considered beautiful and desirable.

This especially plagues our younger generation, but it's not really new. Before the internet there were magazines with glamorous shots of "perfect" women and lots of articles about "slimming." Grapefruit and cottage cheese diets morphed into low-fat, high-fiber, Atkins, Mediterranean, paleo, keto, and so on. Meanwhile our food supply became saturated with high-fructose corn syrup, additives, preservatives, and GMOs—items that make food seem less like food and more like a science project—sabotaging our efforts to eat healthy.

Couple all that with a culture that treats food as a drug, a soother, a weapon, and an entertainment source—and no wonder so many of us are wrecks when it comes to how we approach eating! We're afraid of the food we need to stay alive. We're afraid of being too fat, too skinny, of eating the wrong thing. In a sense, we're afraid of our own bodies, especially when they start to age and change.

How can we overcome all this fear? As I've indicated in a previous chapter, I believe we have to change the way we think. It took me a while, but now I'm committed to the concept of eating to live rather than living to eat. And I've finally reached the place where food doesn't control me. I see it as my source of energy. The right foods can also protect and improve my health. As highlighted in my "What I Eat in a Day" video, I am now able to enjoy food that is pleasurable and satiating. I don't punish myself with over- or underconsumption, and I love the way healthy choices make me feel.

As for the changes in my body that come with age, I try to take a balanced approach. I don't fear these changes or fight against them, but I also don't accept complacency and that attitude of *Oh well, I'm in my fifties (or forties, or seventies), so what should I expect?* Some changes are inevitable, like that loose skin that forms around the knees and elbows—dang it! But many other changes can be avoided or at least delayed. So I'm committed to using resistance training and balance and stability exercises to keep muscle mass, strengthen my bones, and stay mobile. I want to be that upright ninety-year-old who can keep up with her great-grandchildren.

My approach to food and my body changed over the years because I have learned to remove the emotional quotient—including my fears. I rarely weigh myself because I don't need a number to justify what I see. I love my different forms of exercise and discovering new ones. I see myself as lean and healthy, reflective of an emotionally sound woman who wants to feel in control and base her choices on thought and logic rather than a transient feeling like fear.

For me this has been a journey worth taking. I hope my experience can inspire you to go there too—fearlessly.

Fear Issue #3: Sexual Hang-Ups

This is a fun one to address, and I bet you're surprised it made the list. You shouldn't be! Your sexuality matters, and your life will improve if you can conquer your fears in this area, giving up shyness or reserved feelings, understanding what satisfies you, and learning how to communicate your needs with a partner.

Look, certain truths exist here. Past negative experiences can leave us gun-shy. Relationship snags and body-image issues can cause bedroom issues. And certain life stages (menopause comes to mind) can not only pause your sex life but slam the brakes on it! Lack of sleep can leave you wanting to scratch your partner's eyes out should they dare touch you in a seductive way. Hormone fluctuations can cause vaginal dryness, unstable moods, hot flashes, and night sweats—again, not conducive to sexual feelings. No wonder some women want to literally hang up their sexual lives to dry like an old sheet tossing in the wind!

I have learned that you don't have to go through that kind of suffering. No matter what your age or situation, there are options—therapy, supplements, hormone replacement therapy, acupuncture, or all of the above. If you seek help and you don't feel you're being heard or getting the proper guidance, seek other help.

Your general well-being and your sexuality matter. Orgasm is one of life's greatest pleasures, a true gift. Learn how it works for you, let your partner know how to help you get it (a big turn-on by the way), and try something new without fear and shame.

This advice applies to women of all ages but is especially important for those of us of a certain age. You've stopped caring about other things in your life, so don't cover your body with your hands and twist like a pretzel in the light when your love is looking at you. The biggest turn-on is you, proud in your skin, open, receptive, and willing to explore.

Fear Issue #4: Speaking Our Minds

I've earned a right to my opinion, and I know how to articulate it. I believe wholeheartedly in being transparent and authentic at all times. It's so empowering.

I remember times a few decades ago when I would sometimes sit in silence, almost boiling over from not releasing my thoughts or opinions out of fear of being misunderstood, judged, or even laughed at. The younger version of me felt she needed more knowledge and wasn't sure if it or her voice would guide her steadily. Or she was fearful that her honesty would open a can of worms and that addressing certain truths would be too difficult and painful. So she took a back seat to hone another important skill. She became a listener.

Women tend to be good listeners because they notoriously forgo opportunities to speak their minds. Men in general are good speakers because they've always been given the floor. That's why so many women complain that their men don't hear them.

We haven't stopped them from speaking enough to interject our opinions; we haven't stopped them when they interrupted us.

This isn't a male-bashing session, I promise. We love our men. However, we women as a group have let this situation develop, and it's up to us to reverse the course. We must take what's ours, which is a place at the table.

You are bright, capable, and have a feather in your cap that comes from years lived on this planet, and that is wisdom. You have something to offer, and that is your truth, spoken unapologetically and without fear.

If you don't like something, say so. If you *do* like something, say so. If you disagree with something, speak up and explain why. There is nothing cooler for me to see than a woman expressing herself compellingly with dignity, authority, reasoning, and respect—and without fear!

Fear Issue #5: Needing Praise from a Boss or Authority Figure

I see this often, especially in younger people fighting for credit or acknowledgment for a job well done. What I've learned over the years is that a job well done should be its own reward. So many employees fear their superiors and need constant reminders of their efficacy and validity. Some bosses are good at offering praise, but many are silent, with only the occasional interjection. I've worked for tough ones and motivating ones, aloof ones and conniving ones. If I were to base my self-worth at work on the myriad personalities who have been my supervisors, I'd probably be mentally unstable.

I've learned to set a standard for myself and work feverishly to meet or exceed it. The process of setting goals and attaining them is my own pat on the back. It pleases me, and I know it pleases my heavenly Father. What other praise do I need?

I'm not saying you shouldn't seek feedback. I've never been afraid to check in with my supervisors, to ask if I'm meeting expectations or what I can do better. I've also never hesitated to give my input when that's appropriate. I found that most bosses appreciate this. If you work for or with someone who doesn't, someone who makes it extraordinarily difficult for you to shine your best light, then shine where you are at the moment while looking for a better environment.

Don't let the culture at work or elsewhere get you down. Don't let it keep you jumping through hoops, trying in vain to get praise and affirmation. Rise above it just like the cream in your coffee and lift yourself up in praise.

Fear Issue #6: Needing a Child to Like Us

My mother and I laugh all the time about the hate letters I wrote her as a child. She saved every one of them! Those letters were usually fueled by my anger over being denied something I wanted. You would have thought I had the worst upbringing by what I scribed! Running away was brought up on several occasions. I was such a drama queen!

Those letters were my cathartic outlet. My mother understood that and allowed me to express my rage freely without punishing me for doing so. Why? Because she knew I really didn't hate her, and she also knew that the street life wasn't for me.

Children need boundaries, structure, and accountability. Most important, they need love and attention. What they don't need is to be constantly catered to and to always have their way.

If we just try to please our kids and keep them happy, we do them a huge disservice.

We've all encountered parents who behave more like friends than mothers or fathers because they're afraid of not having a good relationship with their children. The dad who drinks too much with the high schoolers at a party so he can seem cool to his son and his friends, or the mom who shares her dating ups and downs with her daughter and solicits her advice and help.

Most parents want more than anything to be liked by their children and to be a part of their lives, but abandoning the boundaries only makes children feel unsafe and unprotected and fosters disrespect.

Sometimes moms and dads have to make hard and unpopular decisions for their children's benefit. That's our job. A young, growing, hormonal mind might not understand those decisions and might react negatively, but the sulking or outbursts are only a child's way of dealing with the emotionality in the moment. Their immature brains are simply not ready to be logical, understanding, and consistent.

Loving my son requires me to get over the fear that he might not like me at times. I need to do what I believe is best for him regardless of how he feels in the moment. I'm even willing to accept the "I hate yous" and the "you're the worsts" because I know darn well our relationship is solid. And I also know that one day we'll be able to laugh about it.

Fear Issue #7: Making and Owning Up to Mistakes

Confession: I used to stand my ground in every argument and do whatever was necessary to be right. I still have that tendency in me, but now I've come to appreciate that we all make mistakes and there's true beauty in acknowledging that. I'm imperfect. We all are! Being able to apologize to others and to myself is a sign of maturity. But if you're a perfectionist, or a recovering one like me, the fear of messing up may be an especially hard one to overcome. The reality that little Miss Perfect maybe made a wrong choice and now has to own it can be hard to digest, but it can also be incredibly liberating.

A great example of this truth is Reshma Saujani, the founder of Girls Who Code, a nonprofit that teaches technical skills to girls and promotes gender parity in tech businesses. A self-proclaimed perfectionist, she spent her early life pushing for big goals—college valedictorian, a career in law, and eventual success in politics. All the while she claims she was playing it safe, not listening to that internal voice hungering to fight for women. Eventually she did run for office and lost but realized that going after her dreams made her feel alive. Her book *Brave, Not Perfect* illustrates that mistakes won't kill us, but perfectionism just might.[1]

No one likes to be wrong. I'm reminded of those *Happy Days* episodes where Fonzie just couldn't get the word *wrong* out of his mouth! It just stuck in his throat: "Rrrrr-rrr." Small word, easy to sound out, but one of the hardest to emit.

Why is it so difficult? The reason is multipronged. There's that awful feeling of knowing we messed up. There's that nagging suspicion that making a mistake means we're not valuable. Then there's addressing how the mistake impacted others and the apology that needs to follow. Not easy. Nobody likes it. But guess what? Once we've accepted that we're not perfect and that no one is, we get better at admitting and even embracing our mistakes.

They're a natural occurrence in life, designed to help us grow by learning from them. And when we practice heartfelt apologies, we give those we hurt a chance to grow by offering forgiveness. In the end, everyone matures from the process.

Fear Issue #8: Getting Older

I really want women to stop being afraid of the next decade in their lives. I've loved every decade of mine more than the previous, and that's because of the wisdom I've gained. We can always seek ways to improve ourselves, and there's joy in that process.

I want to help you begin to see aging as an opportunity to be a better *you* in every way. I can't think of one woman over forty who's said to me, "I'd give anything to go back to my twenties!" Heck to the no! For most of us that decade was riddled with insecurities, uncertainties, and an overall sense of uneasiness about reaching certain benchmarks, like being engaged, married, or having children by a certain age, not to mention cultivating a career.

I find that every decade makes me better, wiser, happier, and more accepting of myself. Yes, we must all face certain truths. At some point our skin won't be as tight. More belly fat will appear. We'll have to manage menopause as well as navigate, redefine, or possibly end relationships, and certain health issues are bound to come up. But as all these things happen, something else does too. We get closer to who we truly are and what really serves us. It gets easier to cast away the loose and tattered sails that no longer move the ship—whatever doesn't bring quality to our lives anymore. We find that we need less to be truly happy.

That's why we women must abolish any fear we might have about aging. It's truly an opportunity to live and breathe in our authenticity and (perhaps) to spoil the grandkids rotten!

Fear Issue #9: The Unknown

None of us knows what will happen tomorrow. We make our plans. We calculate probable scenarios. But we don't really know what the future holds. And for many of us, that reality is a constant source of fear and worry. Our racing minds like to craft all sorts of scenarios—all manner of what-if and how-will-I possibilities. But I guarantee that you can't name a time when worry or fear about what might happen has served you well. It never has, and it never will. I want to encourage you to move past that kind of thinking and change the way you think about your future.

That's much of what this book is about—finding ways to move forward so we don't get stuck in negativity and become paralyzed. We're going to push aside those imagined fear and worry scenarios and rewrite the script on how we operate. As a journalist I've learned there is more than one way to approach a story, and that's true of our life scripts too. Yes, we can write the script with a worst-case-scenario outcome. But you can also write it with the best-case-scenario. Since we really don't know what the future will hold, that second approach is just as valid and far more conducive to healthy, happy, fearless living.

If you often find your mind wandering to the dark side about possible future events and worrying about what might happen, I encourage you to do this exercise. Pick a situation you are facing or think you might face—a new job or loss of your current job, a new relationship or letting go of an old one, a move to a new house or city. Write down your best-case-scenario list of what you think could happen, how the situation could work out well. Then compose a worst-case list, the one driven by imagined worry and fear. Include all the bad things you think could happen.

Now step away from your lists. Giving your mind a break will alleviate your anxiety and help you gain some perspective. When you come back and look at what you've written, your heart rate will probably have dropped, and you'll be seeing things a little more objectively.

Now, read your worst-case list and ask yourself some questions about it. Are your fears based on evidence (have they happened to you before?) or are you just imagining them? And what's the probability that your worst-case scenario will happen? Try to actually come up with a percentage.

Next, consider if there is anything you can do to prevent the worst-case scenario. If so, write down any possibilities. For example, if you're concerned about a failing relationship, write down what you could do to help it succeed: go to church as a couple, seek counseling, spend quality time together, be more intimate, have more meaningful discussions, let the other person feel heard. Seeing these tangible strategies can be an empowering reminder that you're not a victim. You'll also see that even if you exercised all your options and things still didn't work out, you would still survive—and have the satisfaction of knowing you did your best.

Finally, to get the whole situation out of your worried head, get moving. This is so important. Exercise is a known anxiety reducer, so take a walk, throw a Frisbee for the dog, take a kickboxing class. You might try some meditation, too, and definitely spend time in prayer. Afterward, revisit your best-case-scenario list for encouragement. Engage your faith to move toward a positive outcome and fuhgeddabout what's out of your control.

As you can see, exercises like these are part of a well-choreographed dance in a belief system that will have you fighting your fears. Speak words of kindness and prosperity over yourself and block out the naysaying judgment of the past. Your self-talk goes hand in hand with your belief system. The two in tandem can lead to such blessed and rich experiences.

We all know there are no guarantees in life, but we can fight any fear when we activate faith. With confidence and positivity and a belief that God is always extending His hand to lift and comfort and guide us, we can move past anything that holds us back and move into the unknown future with confidence. He is the great enabler and serves as our one true champion. His love for us is immeasurable and abundant. It never fails us, no matter how often we think we've failed Him.

The Hero in Your Own Story

If you want to conquer fear in your life, renew or heighten your faith conversation by offering gratitude for your blessings and seeking forgiveness in any area where you feel you may have gotten off course; then ask away! Ask God for the wisdom and guidance you need to overcome what holds you back. Ask yourself for the courage to trust that He will never fail you.

Pray about it. *Believe* in it! This spiritual shaking leads to an awakening where a new you will shine, the you who pulls back the curtain for the great reveal.

You are the superhero of your own movie, an action-adventure. Truly abandon reality for a moment so you can feel the sensation. It's showtime.

The scene opens with you flying around—beautiful, strong, and oh, so capable. The wind propels you. Your arms are extended, your eyes wide open. Your senses are alive. Your soul is on fire.

You have purpose. You're on a mission, and its outcome will be even greater than the last. Forward is your only direction. Confidence and self-worth fuel your flight. Fear has no power to stop you.

You are lifted higher by your calling to make a difference. To do better, be better. To love more than you ever thought possible.

You are amazing.

Do you see that? Do you feel it?

You are amazing!

SIX

· ·

WHY IT'S TIME TO
GET A HOBBY

WHILE STUDYING BROADCAST JOURNALISM AT the
University of Houston, I also took a deep interest in photography. I took two classes, one in the art department and the other
in the journalism department. Each took a distinct approach to
black and white images, but both involved developing images in
darkrooms with trays of chemicals and using clothespins to hang
up my work while it processed.

I used an old camera my dad had bought in Trinidad in the
1970s, and everywhere I went around town, I looked for something special to capture—something artistic, something that told
a story, something dramatic or daring. I became obsessed with
this hobby, often working in the darkroom until three in the
morning. Getting a print to turn out the way I'd envisioned was
a triumph; I would just stand there and marvel at it.

There was a point where I even considered photography as a

career, but I was drawn even more strongly toward broadcasting. I love and appreciate photography to this day, however, and still look for opportunities to be a shutterbug.

Recently I volunteered my time to photograph a friend's family Christmas card. When I arrived for the shoot, they were all dressed to the nines and had a shiny red vintage car parked in their driveway to add just the right amount of holiday color and panache. The sky was a perfect blue, and their festive outfits matched their joyful smiles.

I better not screw this up! I thought as I clicked away, positioning and repositioning the family in, on, and around the car. Time passed with creativity seeping through every click of the shutter. Thirty minutes later my heart smiled as I toggled through the images in the viewfinder to show them. Even their dog turned out to be a cooperative subject.

A month later that family's Christmas card arrived at my house and was prominently displayed on the fireplace mantel along with cards from other families. Knowing my work had made my friends feel special stirred something deep within me. I definitely plan to create more space in my life to enjoy exploring creative photographic endeavors.

Do What You Love!

Photography isn't my only hobby, of course. If you've visited my YouTube channel (or read this book so far), then you know about my ongoing interest in all things beauty, fashion, and lifestyle. I have always found a way to weave those pursuits into my day-to-day life. I also love to be involved with exercise, nutrition and wellness, gardening, and dance.

A hobby is basically any activity that is done for love and not for money. The line can be blurred, of course, and I know many people who have turned their hobbies into side gigs or second careers. But the hallmark of a hobby is that it gives us a break from our main pursuits in life. And I believe that developing hobbies is crucial to living a balanced and fruitful life.

Hobbies aren't just for fun, in other words. One thing that's beautiful about them is they make us active participants in life, with a fuller range of experience. They help us tap into our creativity and explore what makes us the people we are. As a bonus, they also make us far more interesting to others.

I personally feel an enormous stress release and a sense of calm and joy when I'm pursuing my side interests. I'm stimulated and relaxed all at once, and I'm convinced I'm a healthier and more authentic person because I'm doing something I love.

I think a lot of this goes back to childhood, where many of our passions and interests originate. If you feel your life is hobby-less at the moment, that's a good place to start.

To cultivate these moments, we must create space in our lives. They can be small moments throughout a day or a block of time on the weekend.

Something New and Wonderful

It's amazing where hobbies can originate. One of my most recent ones grew out of a simple conversation with a colleague at work.

We were chatting about exercise, and he shared that he had taken up yoga recently. He's a gym rat like me and had been looking for something new in his routine that would help with stretching his hamstrings. We agreed that men's "hammies" tend to be tight and joked that no one should ever ask a guy to pick up something off the floor. Anyone who does will see an unusual contortion of the human form as the guy makes his way down to the ground, coupled with groaning and grunting to get back up. I laugh just thinking about that image!

Anyway, my colleague shared how much he was enjoying his new yoga class—not quite hot yoga, but very, very warm, about eighty-eight degrees. I told him about my current frustrations with my exercise routine—chronic pain in my neck and shoulders and the constant feeling that my mouth was getting a better workout than my body because of the Chatty Cathies in the gym. I love to talk, really, but I wanted to be in more of a zen mode when I worked out and was having a hard time getting there. So, after our conversation, I decided to give this brave new world of yoga a go.

When I walked into the yoga studio, the smell of the place was a mix of bodies, incense, and fruit. (The juice bar next door was responsible for the orange and banana part.) As I looked around, I noticed something unfamiliar: quiet. The only sound came from the distant blenders whirling the colorful concoctions. The people around me were either preparing for class or leaving, completely wiped out and dripping from what had just happened behind the closed door nearby. I was about to find out what that was.

Pushing through the door, I picked a spot in the middle of the room. I'm usually a front-of-the-line kind of gal, but since I was new, I figured I could use a little guidance from all sides. I laid out my green yoga mat and my pink and green towel with its special grippers on the bottom to keep it in place, then plopped myself down. I noticed people grabbing sturdy foam blocks and straps from the shelves along the wall, and I began to wonder what I had signed up for!

One by one, people scouted the room, looking for the perfect spot to position themselves—sort of like what a dog does before he lifts his leg. Once they found it, I noticed that they did one of three things. Some lay flat on their backs with their eyes closed and just breathed. Others rested their spines on blocks and butterflied their legs. Still others softly chatted with a partner or friend.

I chose to follow the example of the first group. I stretched out in what I now know is called *savasana*, or corpse pose. I didn't know that term in the moment, but within an hour it would bring me to tears.

Class began, guided by soft music and a motivating instructor who named and demonstrated each pose. I eyed my surrounding neighbors, who clearly possessed varying levels of expertise. It didn't matter. Those who were more experienced provided beautiful examples to watch and try to emulate as we pivoted and repositioned on the floor. But there was no sense of competition, no shaming, no comparison of who had bigger biceps or who could bench-press more. Though we all moved together, each of us was alone on our mat, separate in mind, body, and spirit. To each his or her own.

As we proceeded, I found myself in awe of how much strength it took to maintain balance, hold a pose, and transition from one to the other. In Texas terms, that class kicked my butt! By the end my body was fatigued, but not my mind. I felt a sense of complete clarity and presence. Then, to end the class, we all moved into that savasana pose.

In savasana, lying still and flat on your back at the very end of a yoga class, many things can happen. It's a letting go, a release. The breath ebbs and flows in audible waves. The mind is open, free, and expressive. You're encouraged to allow in whatever thoughts and feelings come, pulled magnetically by the hypnotic sounds of the music and the breath.

On that first day, as I relaxed into savasana, I was washed over with emotion, so grateful to God in the moment for the perfect combination of physical exertion and mental peace and space. I was in a room full of people yet alone on my mat, boundaries respected.

And then it came—a rush of vision as clear as the daylight peering in from the long rectangular window. I saw images of my late father. It was as if he were sailing the roaring seas in heaven, joyfully smiling down on me. And he saw me as clearly as I saw him. Before I knew it, my face was being cooled by streaming tears. I was crying in a room full of strangers, and it felt so right.

I was beginning to question if what I really needed that day, what the yoga practice released in me, was more mental and emotional than physical. Was I finally slowing down and shutting off the noise long enough to allow a clear connection to something beautiful inside me? My mind and my body had been clearly vocal about what wasn't serving me. But it took some internal stirring and listening to that voice to finally act.

Taking this one class turned out to be a bold move in my life that continues to bless me to this day with the peace and physicality I was seeking. My yoga practice is my retreat, and I call it mine because I'm alone in a room always, no matter how physically close I may be to others. In that solitude I have united with parts of myself I didn't even know existed.

What was so amazing to me was how creating space for a yoga practice allowed me to revisit old emotions and to visualize. A busy life can bury feelings to the point that we may not even know they're there. Maybe we've tried to shut off some of them because they're painful or we just don't have time to deal with them. But I was grateful in the moment to have that vision and the emotions that followed, to be feeling and not thinking.

Something Just for You

Not every hobby will leave you with tears streaming down your face, of course. But I encourage you to find your own retreat, no matter what it looks like or where it takes you. Our journeys are as unique as the lines on our hands—road maps, really, to a land where we deserve and desire to go.

I do believe something emotional stirs within when we connect to the joyful place inside us that gives rise to our hobbies. Why not make more room for the joy by giving these loved activities more priority?

Keep in mind that you don't have to be an artist to tap into your inner creativity. Your hobby could be anything from cooking to sculpture, swimming to poetry, knitting to indoor rock climbing. There are countless possibilities; you need only to open your mind to them.

We've already established that *you* are your most valuable investment. Letting that reality permeate every cell in your body should convince you that you're worthy of the time to try something new, retry something you loved but set aside, or get more seriously involved in something you've been keeping on the back burner.

What needs to come next? The following have helped me make more room for life-giving hobbies.

Put It on the Calendar

I am a big-time believer in scheduling and making plans. Going through life haphazardly only leads to disorganization and chaos, and more urgent needs can easily cancel out those that are more beneficial. We are busy enough as it is. We can be more effective in balancing what we must do with what we want to do by creating a schedule and sticking to it.

If you want to be an effective scheduler, I suggest writing down what's in your day so you can physically see it. I'm a bit old-school in this way. The calendar on my phone syncs with the one on my computer so that I can pull it up at any time and wrap my head around what's coming up. But I also keep a printed monthly calendar on my desk and write in my scheduled events there. Seeing a month laid out that way helps me better visualize my days and plan. Tight clusters of writing on certain days remind me that I'm overextending and not allowing enough time to cultivate joy and creativity to pursue my hobbies.

I've learned that when I'm overbooked, I'm not in the proper mental space to think creatively or want to try. I need to cordon off space on my calendar and in my mind—space as clear as my Evian water in front of me, open and free like a fall breeze. And to make proper use of that space, I need to be as determined, like a child learning to walk.

Hobbies should be approached with an unabashed willingness

and desire to try, explore, create, succeed, and fail—then do it all over again. That's exactly the mindset that guided our approach to career, parenting, or marriage. In this case the relationship is with ourselves, and the salary paid is in having "all the feels."

Soul-Search and Decide

Once you honor the value of pursuing a hobby and make the time for it, where do you begin? Well, that takes us back to closing our eyes and dreaming of the little girl within us. What did she love to do that stirred her soul? What do you see yourself doing that gives you tingles inside? Or have you watched or read about something new that is speaking to you now?

Start writing a list of possibilities and referencing your passion and talent boards. They will reveal a lot about you, both old interests and potential new discoveries. Don't forget to include current hobbies that still interest you!

You may find that several areas of interest surface in this process and you're not sure which to pick. No worries. Most likely you wouldn't be able to take on scuba certification, Zumba, baking, reading, learning a new language, acting, jewelry making, hiking, and art collecting all at once anyway. Take a little more time and discern which are calling your name the loudest. But keep your list. You may want to return to it someday and try something else.

Don't Give Up Too Easily

Once you've decided where to start, it's time to make a commitment. Any new pursuit—learning to play an instrument, picking up a new language, putting in a garden, whatever—will probably involve a learning curve. You will have success and failure, and nothing will make you feel more like a failure than quitting something you've taken the time to schedule and begin. Hobbies involve not only a time commitment but a mental one as well. Igniting a new interest or reigniting one that has been lying dormant should lead to a slow and steady burn instead of a flameout. Getting that burn going requires patience, perseverance, and maybe digging in the heels a bit.

Now, not everything you try is going to speak to you in the long run. But give it enough time to truly determine if that hobby was right for you or if it's time to pivot to something new.

When I was in my thirties, I decided to take drum lessons. You're shocked, I know! But percussion in music has always really resonated with me. I'm always tapping to the beat of any song, which probably ties in to my love of dance. So I decided the drums would be a great hobby for me. I even invested in my own drum set so I could commit to practicing at home and tackling the homework my instructor gave me.

I went for my first drum lesson, sticks in hand, and began learning my first pattern: "one-and-two-and." When I nailed it, I was thrilled. When I was off—too slow or not reading the music right, like most of the time—that would seriously tick me off. And I have to admit I was off a lot of the time.

Every week I'd go in for my lesson, and just when I felt confident about what I was doing, my teacher would throw in something new that would trip me up and make me feel like I was starting all over. But I was determined. I wouldn't give up.

This went on for about a year and a half—reading the sheet music and banging the rhythm out on the bass, snare, and cymbals. I was getting pretty decent. My goal was to be able to hammer out AC/DC's "Back in Black" all on my own.

One day my instructor was playing in his band at an event I attended. After the first song, they stopped and asked me to come up and play the drums for *that* song! Oh my, there was that "jump off the high dive" feeling yet again. But up the stairs to the stage I went.

I grabbed the sticks, and they looked at me and counted, "Four, three, two, one." *Bah!—Da, Da, Da—Da, Da, Da.* I'm trying my best here to write out how the beginning of "Back in Black" sounds. Anyway, drums and guitar lead off. And I was doing it!

Four minutes and fifteen seconds later, heart in the back of my throat, it was done—as close to Sheila E. as I'll ever get! My percussion was far from perfect, but I banged it out and had this enormous sense of accomplishment for it.

Right around that time, I found out I was pregnant. Eventually my growing belly started protruding into my snare drum and my focus turned to getting ready for a baby. So I gave up my lessons, and eventually I sold my drum set. I never picked up that hobby again, but I'm proud that I committed for as long as I did. I got to play with a band onstage, and you're probably thinking now that I'm one cool chick for it!

End scene. Done.

Community and Connection

Another upside to developing a hobby is becoming part of a new community. Often you will meet new people—an instructor, fellow hobbyists, even entire organizations—who are there for the same reasons you are. This is a wonderful source of potential new friendship and support. You'll meet people who understand why you love your hobby so much, people who can encourage you when you're feeling unsure, people to talk to about your progress and theirs, people who can share what the hobby has done for them and how they were able to get through times when they just felt like giving up.

We all need support, encouragement, and—at times—a gentle push, and that's what you can find in your new community. You will be connecting with people on a primal level, which can lead to higher-quality relationships based on the desire to live an authentic, purposeful, and joyful life.

I mentioned dance as a hobby of mine—it's something I've always enjoyed. Back in 2011 I was asked to participate in a dancing fundraiser to raise money for the Houston Ballet. I learned a cha-cha with my dance partner, who was an instructor. It was exhilarating. I channeled my inner Marilyn Monroe and got to perform a beautiful dance in front of hundreds of fellow Houstonians. What a thrill!

Dance can also be a great way to rekindle the fire with your mate. I know many couples who take lessons together to keep the touch alive in their marriage or regenerate those feelings from yesteryear. It can also be a fun way to exercise, and it's great for any age or stage of life. I met numerous elderly couples when I was dancing regularly who say the activity kept them young and vital.

Sticking with It

Whether it becomes a lifelong passion or a limited pursuit, there's value in sticking with a hobby and analyzing whether it's right for the long term or just for right now. Even though my drumming was a relatively short pursuit, it was fun and left me with a story to tell about trying something new and being vulnerable. Isn't that what we're seeking?

What are we writing in our life book, and how are we filling the pages? Are they consumed mainly with duty, displeasure, boredom, and repetition, or is your story about risk-taking, tenacity, great success, and great failures? Are you *living*?

Your hobbies will certainly help you answer those questions. They are the bright blooms in the garden surrounding the tall trees, adding color, dimension, and beauty.

But here's the fertilizer part that stinks . . .

I was talking with my mom recently, and she acknowledged that she didn't have many hobbies other than going to the gym. That's actually nothing to sneeze at, especially for someone in her eighties, but she was thinking about creative hobbies. I probed a little, and she mentioned that she'd had an interest in art and drawing when she was very young but had never really followed up as an adult. She had, however, maintained an interest in cooking. She and my dad used to make dinner together five days a week. On the sixth day we would have leftovers, and then, on the seventh, we'd usually find ourselves at either the Chinese café or the barbecue joint down the road.

Anyway, one night she invited me over for dinner and made a dish I had always enjoyed growing up—shrimp with rice and bell peppers. She talked about how, being alone, she really had had no desire to make big meals or spend time in the kitchen. She usually made do with a simple grilled chicken breast and a salad and perhaps a baked sweet potato.

That was all good and fine, but our hobby discussion had gotten me thinking, and I suggested it might be stimulating and fun for her to try some new recipes or new ways of making meals. She agreed. Then, right after dinner, I went back to work and was talking with my coanchor. He told me his wife had been loving using her Instant Pot to make meals. They like to eat healthy, so I was interested in all the great things that could be made with this appliance, which is basically an electric pressure cooker with extra bells and whistles.

I went online and checked it out. It looked pretty neat. Then I went searching to see all the different types of meals that could be made, and I was blown away! In two seconds that Instant Pot was in my cart with my mom's address set for delivery.

Like a giddy child, I called her immediately to be on the lookout for a special delivery in a few days. As promised, the Instant Pot arrived. Mom reported that she had unboxed it—then there was a kind of radio silence. No calls, no texts, no emails—so unusual for my communicative mother.

I called the next day and asked what she thought and what would be her first meal to make. There was a pause. "Well, honey, uh, the instruction book is really long, and there's a lot to learn about this thing."

"Oh," I said. "Why not head over to YouTube and see if there are any tutorials on it?"

She started laughing. "Why don't I think of things like that!"

A few more days passed with no Instant Pot discussion. Odd. Finally, feeling like I had made a mistake, I asked, "So did you learn more about it or see any recipes that piqued your interest?"

She replied, "Well, I learned you could really burn yourself if you're not careful, and a lot of the food I saw in the videos was really unhealthy."

At that point I felt like I was the one under pressure. I was ready to drive over to her apartment, box the dang thing up myself, return it to the retailer, and get her a gift card to her favorite restaurant instead. Maybe Instant Pot cooking wasn't the right hobby for her. Or maybe it just needed to be her idea.

Then, out of the blue, she said, "I'm not a quitter, and I'm not giving up on this Instant Pot!" By this point we had been talking so much about that stinkin' pot, it was beginning to feel like a family member, so I was somewhat relieved it wasn't going to be cast aside.

Then she had a brainstorm. "I'm going to Williams Sonoma! I know they have people there who can show me."

Now, at this point you're probably asking, "Dominique, why didn't you just go over there, read the instructions, put the thing together, and show her how to make a meal with the Instant Pot?" Well, because then it wouldn't be her hobby. There's pain in the learning and discovery, and as weird as this sounds, I didn't want to rob her of that. I didn't want to dilute the joy of her making the first meal all by herself.

Anyway, off she went to Williams Sonoma and fell in love with some guy who knew the ins and outs of that pressure cooker. She announced that she would be going there three times a week for lessons! I'm not sure if it was to cook or to hang with a man who could, but either way, she was excited now. She even bought special seasonings and started planning what her first Instant Pot meal would be. Praise the Lord Jesus!

So D-Day finally arrived, and she had decided on a chili recipe. She got the Instant Pot ready, carefully placed it away from any overhanging cabinets because of the steam, got the instruction book out again, and looked everything over. Everything looked great.

She decided to try putting on the lid and then releasing it. Apparently there's a pin that drops for the release, so she wanted to make sure it was working correctly. She grabbed the lid and, per instruction, twisted it clockwise to seal. That worked fine. Then she turned it counterclockwise to open it—again, per instruction. But it didn't open.

She kept working on it. Nothing.

Ten minutes went by, then twenty, then forty. The lid stayed on.

So she called her new best friend at Williams Sonoma, who said, "We close in forty-five minutes; hurry over and we'll figure it out." She rushed out the door to her car and made it to the store in a whopping three minutes. They looked at the pot and twisted the lid to no avail. After giving it a good go, they decided it was defective.

Holy guacamole, I got my mom a defective pot! Now what should I do? Order a new one and wait for delivery, with the potential of all this becoming a major waste of time and a possible traumatic event?

Nope. They took the nonworking Instant Pot and gave her a new one on the spot—and they checked the lid on this one to make sure it closed and opened properly. I love those people! So out the door she went and headed to the grocery store across the street. She got all the ingredients needed for her new recipe and headed home to *finally* make her first meal, now days in the making.

With everything laid out on the countertop and the new Instant Pot ready to be fired up, she realized she had bought the wrong kind of canned tomatoes. I think I would have given up on this whole rotten mess by this point. But no, she headed back to the grocery store and selected the right can.

Back home, she switched on the Instant Pot, and it lit up like the starship *Enterprise*. Mom opened the lid and carefully placed the ingredients inside. And twenty minutes later—voilà! Chili, anyone—with organic shredded cheese and carefully placed baked tortilla strips on the side?

Passion and Pursuit

Yes, there can be humor in hobbies—also, as my mother can attest, stumbles and bumbles. But in the end, as she also attests, hobbies are a blessing. Mom's already looking forward to what she'll make next in her Instant Pot. I hear it will be chicken soup, something I always loved as a kid.

We all have our areas of interest, our unique gifts and talents to be used and celebrated to benefit not only us but potentially the world around us. Some of the greatest people we admire, who created some of the greatest art forms from painting to music, dance to architecture, and even culinary delights, started out pursuing a hobby. Their fulfillment became our enjoyment, and I believe all the greatness in the world began with someone's passion and pursuit.

We were all made with our own unique gifts and talents to cultivate and grow. They can bring so much joy to our lives. Pay close attention to those gifts. They are God's way of showing you where your happiness and creativity will blossom.

A joyful life is one that recognizes and develops those talents, whether they remain hobbies or develop into careers. Whether you're a student plotting your future course or a woman reentering the workforce, analysis and acknowledgment of your divinely inspired abilities will lead to work that never feels like a job and productivity or sheer enjoyment that just flows.

Life is too short not to honor the undercurrent of joy that lies within us.

SEVEN

· ·

THE MAGIC OF MENTORING (AND BEING MENTORED)

NONE OF US GETS TO where we want to be in life alone. We can all go further if we help out one another, and we can all learn from each other in countless ways. That's where mentoring comes in.

We all need mentors. The best way to grow in any area of your life is to identify a person (or people) you admire and ask them to share their own experiences with you and talk you through some of your decision-making. There is so much to be learned from someone who has already walked the path you're on, and they receive just as much joy in helping to guide you.

The Gift of Having a Mentor

Dr. Bob Musburger was a pivotal mentor of mine during my days at the University of Houston. One of my classes with him was

Electronic Field Production. EFP is a television industry term referring to video production that takes place in the field (on location). That class prepared me for the next one, Producing and Directing, where each student produced a thirty-minute show that actually aired on Houston's channel 8 (KUHT), the nation's first public-education television station. Dr. Bob saw a hunger in me and a willingness to stretch and to grow, and he became an invaluable source of guidance in terms of content and direction. I was always passionate about storytelling, and I had an appreciation for images both in still and video form. He saw that, and he took the opportunity to teach me his craft—the art and science of good television journalism.

The show I decided to produce (and host) for channel 8 was centered on the current luxury trends in Houston, which were evolving right before our eyes. A beautiful new mall, the Pavilion on Post Oak, had just opened, and the developers were bringing in a lot of new high-end retailers, breathing new life into the local fashion culture. There was a hair salon there that had originated in France, and the styles women were wearing as they walked out of this salon were the absolute antithesis of the typical "big hair" we see in Texas. They were sleek, refined, and—in my opinion—stunning. There was also a luxury automotive dealer that rented out high-end imports like Ferraris and Maseratis for people to drive around for the weekend. There was no doubt about it—a new level of luxury had arrived in Houston, and I was thrilled to be able to tell that story and even host my own thirty-minute broadcast. Dr. Bob's guidance played a huge role in making it possible, and I was proud of the final product. Having a professor who inspired me, guided me, and showed me how to achieve what I wanted in my stories was a joy.

I maintained contact with Dr. Bob after graduation, and we would touch base every week while I was on the job hunt. He was plugged into the local community, and he would direct me to job openings. Only three weeks after graduation, he told me there was a position at Metro Traffic Control, a traffic reporting company for radio and TV stations. They were looking for a radio traffic reporter. And when talking to the hiring manager, I quickly discovered that he, too, had taken classes from Dr. Bob and felt about him the same way I did. I got the job and thus began my broadcasting career.

Today Dr. Bob and his wife live in the Pacific Northwest, but he still visits Houston from time to time. When he's here, he and I always have a lunch together along with his other mentees and past students.

I acquired another great mentor when I started my job as a disc jockey at Mix 96.5 in 1991. Being a DJ was completely foreign to me, even though I had interacted with DJs as a traffic reporter, with my scripted list of backups, wrecks, and road closures. I got hired based on my energy and my camaraderie with the DJs, but this was a whole different animal, and I faced a significant learning curve.

A DJ has to seamlessly get all the station IDs and branding information out there during their breaks between songs, along with information about the music being played. Once you push the button to start a song, you have to add in some background on the singer or their new hit, maybe tie in a listener's request of it and what part of town they're in, and do all of that in what might time out to twenty-eight seconds before the artist sings. Heaven forbid you step over the vocals! And your commentary has to come across like a normal conversation—with ease and enthusiasm and without sounding like you are reading something.

I began working at the station part-time on weekends and eventually got promoted to the overnight shift, as I mentioned in chapter 4. It was such an incredible opportunity for someone of my age, but it also came with a hefty price. With burnout on the horizon, I really had to stretch to keep my energy and focus. Enter John Clay, the station's music director—in charge of the music selection for each hour. (And you thought the listeners decided what songs were played!)

John would also conduct air check sessions with the DJs on a weekly basis to critique us and help us develop our craft. An air check is a recording of the show without the music—just the disc jockey talking straight through. (There was a special recording device in the control room that recorded only when the DJ's microphone was on.)

Those air checks always happened in John's office, which overlooked the city. But he would be fixated on the blank notepad in front of him while I sat across from him, preparing to be sliced and diced. And so it would begin: play, listen, stop.

"So what did you think of that break?" John would ask.

"Well, I think I was going too fast and sounded like I was reading too much," I would reply.

He would concur and ask me how I could make it more conversational. He would break down what was important to say and what could have been left out and praise the places where I showed my personality.

This went on and on as we examined every recorded break. John had a rule—no more than one page of notes on that legal pad. He felt that anything more would be too much, and believe me, it was plenty!

During one of these sessions, exhaustion and frustration hit me all at once, and I started crying. It was extremely unusual for me to cry in public. I realized I was at the end of my rope and wondered how much more I could possibly handle.

As I tried to dry my tears, John pointed to the door where the talent walked in and out every day, and he said to me, "Do you see that door behind you?" I nodded. "Every time you walk through that door and it shuts behind you, I want you to wipe away your fatigue, your exhaustion, your personal problems, and everything else. The minute that door closes, you have a fresh, new opportunity to start again."

I can't tell you how much that little speech helped me. That door became a metaphor for setting aside negative emotions, fatigue, and any thoughts that could bring me down. Whenever it closed, I had a shift in thinking and renewed confidence in my abilities. And as you learned, I was promoted to a better shift not long after.

John taught me such a valuable life lesson in that. When you're trying to grow your career or struggling in any area where you want to excel, you cannot bring personal issues or exhaustion to the table. And that's the advice I give broadcast students to this day. "Yes, it will be hard. And no, you won't make much money at first, and you'll be asked to do a million things every day. Yes, you'll wonder sometimes how much longer you can sustain your momentum, but you must keep your eye on the prize and your spirits high. Ask to do more. Ask how to be better." Typically it's in those early stages of a career that most people drop off, but the lesson I learned from John—and the lesson I now share—is, "Don't let that be you!"

Honored to Be a Mentor

I believe having mentors is imperative, and I believe that being a mentor to others is equally important. I've been honored to mentor a lot of different students over the years, and I have deeply enjoyed having them come shadow me at the station. I've had many wonderful young men and women do that for a day, a week, or even an entire summer.

One mentee of mine went on to anchor in several different markets. Early on in her career, she married a former KPRC colleague of mine, a reporter who had worked at the station in the early '90s. Coincidentally, he was named my new coanchor in 2020, and she's currently busy raising their two children in Houston after moving here from Dallas. It's been such a blessing to have this long-term relationship and history. I wouldn't have such a great story to share if she hadn't reached out to me for guidance or if I hadn't taken the time to serve in that role.

I take it as a responsibility God has given me to pass along to others the wisdom and practical skill I've gained over the years, to pay it forward. It's beyond fulfilling to watch students take what I've taught them and apply it in their own unique ways. I love seeing them thrive and get to the next level in their careers. And just helping them open their eyes a little bit more and understand the inner workings of the business is a thrill for me. What fun would it be to keep it all to myself?

My dad had this great expression: "Last shirt has no pockets," meaning we can't take anything with us when we're gone. It's so much more satisfying to share the knowledge with others so they, too, can succeed.

I've always seen my YouTube channel as a form of online mentorship, and one letter from a viewer showed me just how powerful that mentorship role can be. This woman bared her soul as she described her walk toward boldness and blessing. The product of a dysfunctional family, she endured years of personal trauma. But she chose to let those setbacks set her up for her choice of career, which involved helping others. She discovered my videos one day while searching randomly for packing advice, then searched through the playlists for more content. In her letter she thanked me for being an example of someone who chooses to develop both inner and outer beauty, and she said that my ways of communicating have resonated with her and guided her in her own journey of relating to others. She even wanted to know if I could offer a class or consultation!

I actually met this beautiful woman when I was in New York to do a makeover on a viewer for *Today with Hoda and Jenna*. She was the first person who approached me after I got out of the car service, heading to NBC. She told me her name and mentioned her letter to me. I immediately knew who she was, and we embraced as if we had known each other a lifetime. She was even holding a sweet sign, as many do, outside the glass walls of the *Today* broadcast. I honestly don't think I can find the words to adequately express the swell of emotion and gratitude I felt in that moment to have connected with my viewer in this way. She and I still communicate, and we've promised each other a lunch date when possible.

In case you're wondering, the viewer chosen from Rockefeller

Plaza for that day's makeover had flown in from Toronto, Canada, to be there. And we've kept in touch too! We text and DM each other often and lift each other up with praise and support.

The warmth and exuberance from all these women—there was even a mother-daughter team who had flown in from South Africa!—only solidified my desire to remind every woman that she is worthy of feeling and being her best. If I could hold your hand, look you in the eyes, and say, "You've got this. You have the necessary tools. Sharpen your pencils, and let's go," I would do it. I'm there for you, cheering you on, and I hope you know that.

Learning from One Another

Have you started to hit the reset button in your life? Are you aiming in a new direction, and has that change left you with a sense of excitement but also uncertainty and a litany of questions? Now's the time to seek the help and guidance of those who have walked the path before you.

Pack away any insecurity you may feel about reaching out and asking another person to mentor you. Even if they say no, they won't see you as incapable or lesser than. In fact, you will honor them by letting them know that their knowledge is valuable to you. You'll be handing them a gift as well as offering yourself one by opening up and being vulnerable. And chances are, they will say yes!

Keep in mind that mentoring relationships can be invaluable in any area of life, not just work. In some cases, they can be lifesaving.

Senior Mentors

If you seek wisdom and knowledge, consider seeking out an older adult whose wrinkles not only reflect his or her years around the sun but also serve as battle scars and badges of honor. The greatest gift we can give seniors is to show that we value them by asking questions and listening with intent.

Older adults are all too often dismissed and disregarded in our society. When we look at other cultures that value their elderly and choose to respect and learn from them, we can see just how wrong our dismissal is. I would encourage you to embrace the older adults in your own life and discover the secrets they have that could inspire and propel you forward. We can honor the previous generations and give ourselves the gift of their wisdom by listening to what they have to say.

I spent a lot of time with my father toward the end of his life. I would sit still, either over the phone or by his side during visits, and listen with great interest as he detailed his childhood and his life during World War II and explained how those experiences shaped the man he became. Those conversations offered me a window to his soul, allowing me to better understand the decisions he had made and the pathways he had chosen. Dad's stories also provided a different perspective on life in general, a sense of regret for things I may have taken for granted and a yearning for a time when certain aspects of life were better than they are now. I'm so grateful that I took the time to listen while I still had my father with me. Let's not let our parents leave this earth without connecting as deeply as possible with those who dared greatly to bring us into this world. We owe it to them and ourselves.

Mom Mentors

As you're seeing, mentors aren't just for careers and hobbies. They're invaluable for almost any aspect of life. Motherhood is a case in point. An experienced "mom mentor" can be a powerful ally to a younger mother, especially if she resists judgment or criticism, simply sharing what worked for her and offering a shoulder to cry on when the going gets tough.

One of the biggest fallacies on this earth is that motherhood is all fairy tales and rainbows. When I was pregnant, people painted such an idealistic picture of parenting. I would have really benefited from a healthy dose of realism. Since my son had colic, there was no sleeping in my house for a good eight months. I also had a dose of postpartum depression, a totally foreign experience for this glass-more-than-half-full kind of gal.

During that difficult time, I just couldn't bear to see a smiling, sleeping, happy baby. I know that sounds horrible, but I just couldn't relate, and I was convinced that every mom I met was doing a better job at parenting than I was. It wasn't until I started sharing my story of fatigue and sadness over how difficult it was that I finally started hearing about other mothers' struggles. It was as if everyone had been keeping the reality a big secret, and no one wanted to burst the bubble.

As it turned out, very few of the moms I knew had "perfect" babies, and many were dealing with issues similar to mine— maybe not to the same extent, but they could relate. I felt such a sense of relief that I wasn't doing any wrong and what I was experiencing wasn't my fault. Knowing I was not alone took a huge load off my shoulders.

All I wanted in those dark days, more than anything in this world, was for my little guy to feel good and be happy. However,

I forgot that I needed the same! I completely neglected my needs as a working mom during this time, stumbling through life with frayed nerves and little sleep. I could truly have benefited from counseling, connection, and a night nurse! And I desperately needed a motherhood mentor.

I know better now, of course. Never again will I fall on my sword in the name of trying to portray that everything is okay with me if it's not. Today I'm the first to say that, yes, a child is God's greatest gift, but parenting can be the hardest thing you ever do. You will be tired a lot of the time. Some days will be easier than others. And it's okay to reach out and get help if things don't feel quite right.

How to Be a Great Mentor

How do you take someone under your wing as a mentee and share your knowledge and experience with him or her? Simple. Just keep your eyes open and look for the opportunity. If you have an area of expertise, look for opportunities to share that expertise.

If you're a lawyer, offer up yourself or your firm for internship positions or reach out to a school with prelaw students you can teach for a day. If you're proficient at crochet or cookie decorating, offer to teach a class at a local church, a high school, a shelter for abused women, or just a group of young women in your kitchen. Or, if you're a tech whiz, you can offer to help seniors learn to code. (Mentorship doesn't always need to involve older people teaching younger.)

Mentorships can be formal or informal. Many schools,

corporations, and other organizations offer formal mentorship programs to match up willing mentors with those who need their help. But as we've already seen, informal mentoring relationships can make a huge difference as well. We all have gifts and talents to share, so we must seek out those looking to attain the same knowledge.

Here are some general guidelines on how to be an effective mentor.

- **Let them see you in action.** People generally learn more effectively by seeing rather than hearing, so a mentorship that allows the mentee to watch you work will generally be more effective than a lecture or a talk. I found that when broadcast journalism students visited me at the TV station for a day and watched a day in my life, so to speak, they were better able to determine if the field was for them or not. There's so much more to glean by seeing a mentor in action first and then following up with the questions. Mentees can actually visualize their future life in the moment and get a sense for how that feels. I've had many mentees tell me after one day that the news business wasn't for them. How great to figure that out so quickly instead of wasting four years of college study!

- **Aim to inspire as well as inform.** I believe that most people want to make an impact and leave their mark. I also believe that it's our role as mentors to show how they can do that, not just describe the details of what we do. For example, I could have described my TV news line of work in two possible ways, either (1) "I assess and analyze the news of the day, cowrite my copy, and deliver the content from a news desk via teleprompter," *or* (2) "I have the honor of writing and delivering the news of the day, selected by what will be most impactful and useful, to inform my community about the world around them so they can feel safe, empowered, and aware." Now, which description would motivate you to become a broadcast journalist? Ding, ding, ding! That's right—number two. Mentors need to inspire through actions *and* words.

- **Don't expect a copycat.** It's only natural—and even commendable—for mentees to put their own spin on what they're learning. No two people are alike, so no two approaches will be either. Their way may be better, or it may not be. We must accept and honor individuality in the process while offering our words of wisdom about what has or has not served us well. If your mentee seems to be veering off course, whether you approve or not, you will usually do best to let it be. There are natural checks and balances along the way to correct people if they veer off course. It's the natural way to learn—by reaping rewards and suffering consequences. A mentor cannot and should not expect to break every fall and prevent every fail. God uses those failures to help us grow. Let's not get in the way of that important process for our mentees.

- **Clarify expectations and accept responsibility.** Don't enter a mentor/mentee relationship casually, thinking you can just stick your big toe in the water. To really make a difference, you must honor any commitment you make. If you start and don't finish or if you lose steam along the way, you send the signal that the mentee isn't worthy of your time. Losing a mentor prematurely can be a big blow to someone's self-esteem. Just as a teacher has a course they must teach for a semester or year, it's a good idea to establish the terms, parameters, and expectations of a mentoring relationship in the beginning. These can be renegotiated if necessary to accommodate changing needs, scheduling, and the like, but there should be a mutual agreement of commitment, time, and output from both sides.

- **Don't stop being a mentee.** You haven't hit your ceiling, and there's always room to stretch and learn. Life never sits still, nor will your industry or area of expertise. Do your best to stay current and learn the new ways of operating, even if you still prefer the old. Human beings stagnate when we stop learning; our brains need constant challenge to keep us young at heart. Your role as a mentor can always grow if you're willing to grow as well.

- **Get 'em when they're young.** It's been said that one in three young people will grow up without having a mentor.[1] Volunteering to take a youngster under your wing is an awesome opportunity to shape a young life. You're probably aware of national mentoring programs like Big Brothers Big Sisters of America, which pair children, teens, and young adults with older mentors. What an awesome opportunity to help mold someone's future! My colleague and former coanchor Khambrel Marshall sits on the Houston board of this wonderful organization. I've deeply enjoyed his stories of mentors making a difference and seeing that warmth through his eyes. And did you know there are twice as many boys waiting to be paired as girls? Ladies, grab your men and let them know there are young boys in your community who could benefit from their care and willingness to share. The need is great to shape the outcomes of these young lives, and this may be a great place to start if you're looking to make a difference.

Mentoring in Your Own Family

If you're a parent, then you know there's no greater gift than being a mentor to your own child. I cherish the times my son comes to me for advice and we have one of those open, honest, heart-to-heart conversations, the ones where we're really listening to each other and being heard.

As parents, our actions, decisions, thoughts, and emotions can be mentoring tools, providing teachable moments. When Styles was growing up, he witnessed a mom who worked tirelessly to be present for him, love him unconditionally, educate him, respect him, and make him feel safe. And he learned firsthand that all of this was possible with a working mom. I just had to work harder, stretch more, and sacrifice more. All you working moms know that. There's no such thing as perfect parenting, just being able to say that you gave it your all.

And how about mentoring opportunities for a stepparent? The possibilities are abundant in this relationship. A bonus mom or dad is an extra adult in a child's life who can bring something new to their world. You're close enough to know what's going on, but because you're not the parent, you have a unique perspective. You can add something extra, something special. And maybe you have a skill set or knowledge base that appeals to your bonus children.

Whether it involves a job, an area of expertise, a family connection, or just shared life, the role of mentor and mentee is an incredibly fruitful one. Our willingness to spend the time, answer the questions, and dole out knowledge can help set someone's future course, or at least their areas of interest. And our willingness to listen and learn gives honor to those we're learning from. It's a rich source of growth in their lives and our own.

In my mind mentorship is not optional. It's one of the best ways I know for us all to connect and grow.

· ·

EIGHT

KEEPING IT CLASSY

WHAT'S THE BEST COMPLIMENT YOU can think of?

For me, being labeled a "class act" would just about do it.

Maintaining a certain level of class and sophistication in how I look and how I behave is incredibly important to me. And judging from the comments on my YouTube channel, I believe it's important to many women too.

Keeping it classy shows that we care for and value ourselves and others. If we want to be treated with respect, then we must first be respectful. We must present ourselves in the best light possible, not only for our self-esteem but also for the type of world in which we wish to live.

The actress Audrey Hepburn, in my opinion, was the ultimate example of what it is to be classy. She is widely associated with the following quote, which she once read out loud to her family and which her son read at her funeral:

For attractive lips, speak words of kindness.

For lovely eyes, seek out the good in people.

For a slim figure, share your food with the hungry.

For beautiful hair, let a child run his fingers
through it once a day.

For poise, walk with the knowledge you'll never
walk alone.

SAM LEVENSON[1]

What a lovely lens with which to view life and beauty!

I've always held Audrey Hepburn in the highest regard. In fact, I have a painting of her in my home, and I sit right in front of it for many of my YouTube tutorials.

I've been asked so many times where I got the painting, and I just have to share the story with you. Several years ago my TV station demolished its 1970s-era building and erected a new, state-of-the-art one in the parking lot behind it. Before the demo work began, management sent out an email saying that if there was any artwork on the walls we wanted, we could go for it. Well, that Audrey Hepburn painting had been in the ladies' restroom for goodness knows how long, and I had always loved it. The minute that email appeared in my inbox, I beelined for the restroom, grabbed Audrey off the wall, and stashed her by my desk until I took her home at the end of the day. Of course, I did all of that in my high heels with *great* poise and composure!

I often joke that I was born in the wrong era. I'm so drawn to the grace, the timeless glamour, and the elegance of old Hollywood. Along with Audrey Hepburn, I admire Sophia Loren, Raquel Welch, Marilyn Monroe, Katharine Hepburn, and so many others. While I'm thrilled with the advances we've made since then in terms of opportunities for all women, I do think we would do well as a society to infuse just a touch of that old Hollywood charm into our day-to-day existence.

That's not to say there aren't modern-day examples of that charm and class. When I consider the celebrities of today, I am captivated by Charlize Theron. She epitomizes elegance, no matter what she's wearing or how she styles her hair. In fact, she's been through an enormous number of different hairstyles and colors, and she's not at all afraid of change. She's been a style icon of mine for years, and I love that she's willing to take risks yet always remains classy in her presentation. She is quoted as saying, "I don't believe in charmed lives. I think that tragedy is part of the lesson you learn to lift yourself up, to pick yourself up and to move on."[2]

Angela Bassett, too, is a beautiful example of class. Stunningly beautiful and a Yale graduate, she is known for portraying strong, iconic women, such as Tina Turner, Rosa Parks, and Ramonda in the *Black Panther* franchise. Bassett admitted in a 2001 interview that she liked such "real woman" roles and added, "That's the image that I like to put out there, and those are the parts I'm attracted to. But not iron-fist kind of strong, just self-assured. I'm nice too."[3]

Smart and beautiful. Strong and self-assured but "nice." That's the kind of class I aspire to. Don't you want it too?

Staying Classy in Hard Times

Class really shows itself when life gets difficult and things go wrong. We can choose to fall apart at the seams in those circumstances or we can summon the grace to manage the crisis, adapt, carry on, and hopefully find the lesson in what has happened.

Summoning that kind of grace during an unprecedented disruption like the COVID-19 pandemic proved to be challenging for so many of us—me included. Everything changed, almost overnight—family life, work life, church life, entertainment—and we all were left grappling with what those changes would mean for us. And Zoom practically became part of our families.

So I appreciated an insightful conversation I had with my TV agent, Ken Lindner, at the beginning of 2021. Kenny has been my "career choreographer" from the get-go, representing me in the news business since I started in 1994. And even though I've stayed in the same market and at the same station my entire career, having an agent who's a lawyer comb through every contract to protect me and get the best deal for me has been invaluable.

On this particular day, Kenny and I were talking about how the industry has changed over the years and how videoconferencing calls kept the conversation going in broadcast television during the COVID pandemic, when people weren't in studio anymore but guests still needed to be booked for segments. He even pointed out that Zoom interviews will probably still be common by the time this book is released in the spring of 2022 because the Zoom platform has provided easy access to experts, guests, authors, and celebrities without the expense of travel or safety issues. He projected that I would get booked over Zoom to promote my book in markets where I might not have had a presence before. I was excited about this upside of the pandemic—and trust me, I've been searching for the silver lining since January 2020!

Even though I was still able to show up to work and broadcast out of KPRC during the pandemic in a very socially distanced way, many people behind the scenes in our organization, those who didn't need to be in an office setting to get their jobs done, ended up working from home. Video conferences were booming, and this was uncharted territory when it came to what it meant to look, dress, and act professional. Fashion terms like *athleisure* and *luxe leisure* came into prominence for good reason. There was a complete loosening of the lifestyle simply because people weren't having to put on their fancy suits and sheath dresses to go to work. Work was at home, but it was still work, and people found it hard to know how to present themselves.

A Zoom Call Protocol

I saw a new need developing here based on my mantra of "keep it classy." I could sense how this relaxing of standards could potentially affect how people were seen within a company, how they were assessed in hiring interviews, and, most importantly, how they felt about themselves. So, I set about developing a Zoom-call protocol video to guide workers who were struggling with this issue. Here are some takeaways that might help as we all try to figure out this new normal.

Takeaway #1: Stay Level-Headed

To really help your confidence and how you feel you look on your device's camera, keep it at eye level or slightly above. Here's why this is important. If your laptop, tablet, or phone is on your desk and you're sitting in the chair, the device will be lower than your face and will give you an up-the-nose, three-chins look.

To avoid this, you need to get your device up to eye level. Put something like a stack of books or a small box underneath your device to raise it. That way you can look straight into the camera and not have it catch you at an unflattering angle. Another trick is to raise it even slightly above eye level. Photographers have long known that shooting slightly down at a subject has a slimming effect. Why not make it work for you?

Takeaway #2: Look 'Em in the Eye

Have you noticed how tiny the camera is on a laptop and how big the screen is? When you're on a Zoom call, the temptation is to look all around the screen and take in the Brady Bunch grid in front of you. That's fine when someone else is talking. But when it's your turn, looking at the people on your screen gives the impression that your eye is wandering and you're not really focused on what's going on.

You'll look more engaged if you actually look at that tiny little camera at the top of the device. That's what gives you eye contact with your audience. Aren't we always saying to children, "Look me in the eye"? The same principle applies here.

It's an unnatural feeling to talk into that tiny camera when your instinct is to look at the person on the screen, but trust me, it comes across as if you were looking straight at them. Here's my trick to help you. Take a little piece of tape or a sticky note and put it next to the camera. You can even make a smiley face on it as a reminder of where your eyes need to be when talking. Look at the tape, and you'll be looking your audience in the eye. You may have to divert your attention a little bit during a presentation, and that's fine. But when you're done—eyes on that lens.

Takeaway #3: Sound Like a Pro

I know it seems odd, but when you sound better you actually look better! And what you need to sound better is a good microphone. There's a huge difference between using the microphone that's built into your device versus a plugged-in microphone or wireless earbuds with a mic.

If you do a lot of video conferencing, a quality audio device is worth the investment. You really don't have to spend a lot to boost your sound quality with a USB external mic or Bluetooth earbuds. Think of it as creating your own at-home studio!

If that's not in the cards for you, the best thing to do is keep that computer close to you to help cut down on distracting ambient noise. Turn off TVs and other electronics, warn your family that you're about to have a meeting and need quiet (good luck with that!), and try to isolate yourself in the quietest part of your house.

Takeaway #4: Let There Be Light

As someone who has been in the TV business most of her life, I can categorically say that lighting is everything! But lighting can be an issue when we're working remotely. Too many of us end up looking like shadowy, ghostly figures on those video conferencing screens. Let's address why that is.

First, the light that comes from a device screen is usually a shade of blue that tends to make us look washed out and somewhat sickly. A quick remedy is to shine some warm light on your face. You can do this by placing an illuminated incandescent bulb directly behind your device or by using a clip-on ring light or computer light on a warm setting. These are widely available at electronics stores, big-box stores, and online.

I like placing my computer near a window so I have an even wash of natural light on my face as well. But watch out for back-lighting, which is what happens when the window is behind you instead of in front of you or to the side. That's how you become an outline of yourself.

Finally, be on the lookout for bright overhead lights. Any light that comes straight down on your head is just going to make you look hollow under your eyes and cast unwanted shadows on your face. There's a simple remedy for that, of course. Just switch off the overhead, switch on the clip-on, and smile into that camera. With a little preparation, you'll look like you're on a TV news set!

Takeaway #5: Do a Background Check

Trust me, when your camera is on, everyone is looking not only at you but at what is going on behind you. Is the dog chasing its tail? Are the kids fighting over toys? Is a computer screen with sensitive information visible or a scattering of dirty coffee cups?

An occasional interruption by your child or your puppy might be cute and understood by colleagues, but these should be *very* occasional. Even if you're working at home, you want your total presentation to be professional.

If you can, try and maintain some distance between you and the background. That will give a nice sense of depth and be more visually pleasing than a featureless wall directly behind you. But do pay attention to distracting items; you want the focus on you, not the knickknacks on the shelf. And take the time to ensure that everything looks tidy and organized. Having clutter behind you speaks volumes about how you live your life at home and translates into how you're working from home. You don't want to give the impression that you're distracted, disorganized, and not all in.

Takeaway #6: Don't Forget Your Hair and Makeup

Getting your makeup right for work-at-home video conferencing can be a little tricky. Do too much and you might seem a little out of touch with what's going on in the world. Do too little and you won't look professional. A natural makeup application with nude and muted colors will look best and give you a polished but not overdone look.

A couple of my YouTube videos might help you strike the right balance here. One of them is my "Out the Door in 2 Minutes Makeup Routine," and the other one is "Simple Makeup Tips to Look 10 Years Younger." Who doesn't want that—especially now, when all of this aggravation can age us?

When it comes to your hair, make sure you don't look like you just rolled out of bed! At the very least, make sure your hair is clean and run a brush through it before going online. You don't have to overdo the styling with big curls and gallons of Aqua Net. An easy way to look classy if your hair is longer is to slick it back into a clean, classic ponytail.

Takeaway #7: Watch Your Wardrobe

Some common sense should apply here. Tank tops and spaghetti straps generally look unprofessional. Loungewear or workout wear may be too casual. Pajamas—don't even think of going there! I don't recommend the other extreme either, except in very unusual circumstances. It's not hard to find a happy medium that strikes the perfect tone of what I call easy professionalism. It could be just a simple silk blouse or a nice button-down top in a flattering color. Remember, nobody knows what's going on below, so keep it comfortable and loose if you'll be sitting for a while.

When it comes to jewelry, think *the smaller the better.* Anything too shiny or moving around will distract from what you're saying. I like to stick with a thin necklace and a simple pair of earrings. That combination shows that you made the effort but are conscious of what can take away from your message.

Takeaway #8: Watch Your Mouth

How you speak and your choice of language says so much about you. In a home environment there may be a tendency to relax some barriers and loosen restrictions that may still need to be there. Beware of unleashing any curse words or using language you wouldn't normally offer up in your work environment. That includes whining and complaining! I know there were many trials and tribulations during the pandemic months and beyond, and some of us got in the habit of using Zoom to vent and commiserate. But that kind of conversation is best held with a friend or a counselor. Let's not loop in our coworkers with how bored or how mad and frustrated we are with our personal or global situation. We still have to keep that line of professionalism, so know what to say when and to whom and be the light that's so desperately needed in a dark time.

I don't know about you, but my mind keeps drifting off to the possibilities of getting back to normal—when we can safely live outside the home and the computer monitor and roam in the outside world without masks and social distancing. Just the idea of dressing up for a gala or getting dolled up for date night warms my heart. It's slowly but surely happening in some areas. And as I think of meeting people face-to-face without screens, masks, or social distancing, I'm thinking more and more about what it means to present myself with class.

The Elements of Class

To me, class is a composition of the physical, mental, and spiritual. Not one aspect dominates; all three intertwine. Class shows in the way we dress and do our hair and makeup, the way we interact with others, even the way we think and feel. It shines in our personal style and our behavior.

As I see it, we all have a number of tools at our disposal to keep it classy in all these areas of our lives. If you're looking to breathe some refinement into your own life and present yourself to the world as a classy, sophisticated woman, this is a good place to start.

A Classy Wardrobe

My rule of thumb when it comes to wardrobe is to reference what French women are wearing. When it comes to class, style, and sophistication, the French usually nail it. And the essence of the French approach to wardrobe is "less is more." You always want to think sleek and simple. And you want to focus on quality rather than quantity. Instead of a closet full of pieces that you may not even wear, focus on building a "capsule wardrobe" of beautifully tailored garments made of quality, high-end fabrics.

And yes, putting together that classy wardrobe can be pricey, especially if you buy new and pay retail. But I almost never do that! As I mentioned in an earlier chapter, I'm a big proponent of resale shopping, which is how I find all my higher-end items. It pains me to pay full price for anything, especially when there are so many fabulous secondhand options, both locally and online. The fact that those quality pieces will look good much longer than a collection of "throwaway clothes" makes them more affordable in the long run.

And keep in mind that you don't have to buy your wardrobe all at once. Start with one good piece and supplement it with lower-priced options. Then gradually, as you are able, replace your lower-quality items with more good pieces. Have a plan and build your classy wardrobe a piece at a time. You'll be surprised how quickly it comes together and how great it makes you feel.

When putting together a capsule wardrobe, think of classic pieces that will mix and match well—perhaps black wool-blend slacks; black pencil skirt; white button-down blouse; black blazer; patterned blazer; red dress; white, blue, or black jeans; light cashmere sweater; black pumps; black boots; tan pumps; tan boots; camel-colored wool coat or trench coat; black pleather jacket; one neutral purse and one black purse; and black sunglasses. Any combination of these essentials, and you can't go wrong.

Once you've created your basic wardrobe, you can go ahead and add some spice with bolder wardrobe pieces. But proceed with caution. You might love your red dress, red suit, red pair of pumps, and bold printed scarf, but don't wear them all at once! Pick one of your beautiful red pieces and keep the rest of your look simple and minimalistic.

The same basic principle applies to your jewelry. For example, a single-strand gold chain necklace, light layered necklaces, or a little choker; gold or silver hoop earrings; perhaps a statement watch or bracelet; your engagement and wedding band or another favorite ring. And again, don't wear all your jewelry at once. Give the eye one area of focus. If you wear a larger necklace, maybe you go without earrings. Or if you choose the hoops, lose the necklace.

That's not to say that you can't have fun with your jewelry or throw in some personality with signature pieces. But if you do, keep the rest of your look simple. Such attention to balance is the hallmark of a classy presentation.

The rule of balance is helpful to remember when you're putting separates together too. For instance, if you're going to do a wider-leg pant, pair it with a fitted top. If you're wearing a skinny jean or a straight pant, look for a looser or blousy top. You want to give the eye one thing to focus on.

Pay close attention to what flatters your shape. God made us all differently, so learn what styles enhance your body lines and celebrate those with quality pieces. Make sure they fit well, and have them altered if they don't. Gaping waistbands, pant hems that drag the floor, plackets that don't button right—all can be remedied with a visit to a tailor or dressmaker. Clothes that are too small or too large will throw off the symmetry of your look. And it's hard to look classy with clothes that just hang on your frame or with skin-tight clothing that leaves nothing to the imagination.

Taking good care of your wardrobe is essential to maintaining that classy look. You simply can't look sleek or sophisticated in clothing that is shabby, stained, missing buttons, or wrinkled. Look through your closet regularly to keep on top of problems.

Keep your iron or steamer at the ready, and if you're not handy with a stain stick or a needle, find someone who can help you. A collection of classy, high-quality clothing is a significant investment, but with proper care it will last you many years.

By the way, you'll notice I haven't included exercise wear and casual wear in my descriptions here. That doesn't mean a classy woman can't wear jeans, shorts, yoga pants, hoodies, or the like! By all means equip yourself with the clothing you need to pursue your interests and be comfortable at home. But even then, you can benefit by keeping the principles of a classy wardrobe in mind. Good fabric, good fit, simplicity, and focus will add a touch of class to almost any outfit, and you'll look great wherever you go.

Classy Hair

There are many different ways to achieve classy-looking hair, many different styles that contribute to that confident, well-kept look. But whatever the style, classy hair is always healthy-looking hair. Frayed ends or overprocessed color will keep you from looking your classy best. To keep that healthy look, get a trim on a regular basis and invest in products that enhance your specific hair type and issues. There are so many wonderful ones available—mousse for volume; gels, pomades, and conditioning treatments to tame the frizz; shampoos to pamper thinning or damaged hair; special products for Black hair. Your stylist is a source of great information when it comes to both product and style, and the internet can be a gold mine as well.

Classy hairstyles should suit the wearer's face shape, lifestyle, and hair type as well as the occasion. If you love longer hair, for instance, that's great. Just keep it in good shape and make sure the overall look isn't dragging your face down. I personally love updos; I think they're very chic. A low ponytail or bun at the nape of the neck can be beautiful and classy. So can a sleek bob, a close-cropped afro, a cascade of loose waves, or a gathering of shining braids. There's nothing wrong with having fun with your hair and following trends, but keep it within certain parameters. Keep it simple, and keep it classy.

Hair changes as we age, and our choice of a classy style may change as well. Many older women I know are letting their beautiful natural gray come in, while others continue to color theirs. It's a matter of personal preference, and I encourage you to do whatever speaks to you.

I *have* noticed that when a mature woman brings her hair up to her collarbone or above, it's like an instant natural face-lift. You can save yourself a trip to the plastic surgeon just by cutting your hair and adding some long, loose layers for movement. We've all seen those transformation videos where it looks like another person emerged three hours later! That's the power of a good, classy hairstyle.

Classy Makeup

The same rules of focus and balance that we considered for wardrobe apply to makeup too. If you're going for a bolder eye look, keep a light and neutral lip. Or if you're going to do a bright red lip, then downplay the eyes. Give people one thing to look at and one thing only. Too much heavy makeup, cakey foundation, and bright color everywhere just detracts from your natural beauty and can take away from who you are. You don't want your makeup to scream *Makeup!* You just want it to enhance your beauty.

I find that as we mature, we need less makeup. Anything too heavy can actually make us look older, accentuating the issues we are trying to cover up.

That's why a good skin care regimen is a must, to get that beautiful natural glow that makeup just cannot give. There are many foundations for mature skin that won't settle into every line and wrinkle and will promote that dewy look we all want. What excites me is seeing how cosmetics and skin care companies are pivoting, not only recognizing the size and scope of this mature market, but responding to our demand to be celebrated as savvy consumers who research products and are willing to spend money on quality.

As a side note, I believe it's imperative to have models reflect the demographic. Nothing irks me more than seeing a twenty-year-old cast in a wrinkle-cream ad. She may be great in an Urban Outfitters commercial, but leave the wrinkle treatments to us mature gals.

I have noticed that the younger generation is wearing less makeup anyway and is focusing more on skin care. That's why we've seen an explosion in the skin care game. Young and old alike want great skin. That's where it all starts. Makeup application is just the icing on the cake—and don't overfrost!

Classy Posture

Next on my list is the way you carry yourself. This is so important to a classy look! Good posture lengthens and elongates; stand up straight and you can look like you've lost five pounds. And there is just something striking about seeing a woman walk into a room with her head held high, her shoulders back. Her posture makes her look self-confident, and there's nothing more attractive—or classy—than confidence. More than wardrobe, makeup, hair, accessories, anything else—if a woman carries herself well, the rest just falls into place.

One key to good posture is simple awareness. Get in the habit of checking yourself in the mirror—from the front and then from the side. See if your head is in alignment with your spine, your shoulders low and gently pulled back. Be mindful of how you are seated at a table or behind a computer, how you're standing and walking. The more you think about it, the better your posture will become.

If you notice a tendency to slump or slouch, I suggest you do some research into ways you can fight that tendency and correct that posture. The internet is full of articles and videos that can help. Physical therapists and other professionals can help as well. Ergonomic furniture and devices may be worth the investment. And a well-balanced exercise routine can make a huge difference. I've found that my yoga practice is invaluable for helping me keep straight and strong. Dance classes help too. But anything that develops your core in a balanced way can help in your efforts to develop better posture.

One posture corrector I especially love is to lie down on a carpeted floor or mat and place a small rolled-up towel under the upper part of your back, about where your bra strap hits. Then cactus your arms out to the side, let your head fall to the mat, and rest there for a while. The towel pushes your upper back up and allows the neck area to reposition and straighten. If practiced daily, it can correct poor posture. As a bonus, it feels great.

Keeping your posture aligned can actually make you feel better in many ways. When you carry yourself well, you usually experience less tension and pain in your shoulders and back and are able to take deeper, more satisfying breaths through your nose. This in turn nourishes your brain with oxygen, leaving you more energized and alert, and expels waste material in the form of carbon dioxide.

Good posture, in other words, is good for you. The fact that it makes you look classy is a fabulous bonus.

Grace

Up to this point, we've been looking at ways to project class on the outside—wardrobe, hair, and the like. But as I said in the beginning, class is also a projection of who we are on the inside, and how we behave is an expression of that inner classiness.

How does a truly classy woman behave? For starters, she exudes *grace*. That's a word with multiple meanings, but one of them is "courteous goodwill."[4] That's the kind of grace I want to focus on here. To me, grace means handling yourself with courteous goodwill in any situation, including those that are tense and uncomfortable.

This is a biggie for me. We as a society have seen a big shift away from behaving graciously and toward acting out and expressing our opinions in any way we want. The result, the way I see it, has been a coarsening of our culture and a general lack of civility and class. We're seeing all manner of foul language, slander, and degrading behavior—even violence. And let's be honest, that behavior is not going to move society forward or shine God's best light on those around us. Behaving graciously will. So let's zip the potty mouth, discipline our behavior, and control our emotions.

Yes, of course we all are entitled to our individuality, to our unique opinions, ideas, and feelings. But what I want to encourage is the ability to express our feelings, thoughts, and opinions with grace. A classy woman will listen without interrupting and offer ideas without demeaning others or putting them down. She keeps her speech civil and even—never harsh, overly confrontational, or laced with profanity. She supports her opinions with facts, logic, and reason and doesn't let her emotions run away with her. And if somebody doesn't agree with her, then she'll gracefully agree to disagree.

I think that we women, especially, need to understand the difference between a thought and a feeling and put a buffer between our emotions and our behavior. One of the biggest frustrations women experience in our society is being judged as too emotional. The best remedy for this is for us to learn to temper emotion with logic and to step away from situations that will leave us acting out emotionally with only regret to follow. There's nothing wrong with disengaging from a conversation or situation, giving the situation some thought, and returning with a reply that comes from a place of grace.

Knowledge

A classy woman is a knowledgeable woman. She values her mind, and she is always eager to enrich it. She soaks up knowledge like a sponge and enjoys sharing it with like-minded people. Well-read, cultured, and aware of what's happening in the world around her, she holds her own in conversation without being overbearing. (She's knowledgeable, not a know-it-all—secure enough in herself that she doesn't have to be *right* all the time.)

None of us, of course, can know everything about everything, and a classy woman is well aware of that. When conversation meanders toward a topic about which she's unfamiliar, she takes that opportunity to listen, learn, and analyze. She asks questions and does her own research, building her knowledge base around topics that intrigue her.

My own areas of interest are health, wellness, relationships, parenting, and psychology, so I invest a lot of my time into researching them. I want to arm myself with information, theories, ideas, and experiences pertaining to subject matter that speaks to me. I also make a point to be well versed in the news. That was a professional requirement, of course. But a knowledge of current events also gives me a good subject base to initiate conversation and hold my own in a lively discussion.

Classy Behavior

In thinking about how we present ourselves to the world, we should pay special attention to the way we behave, especially the way we treat others. Kindness, thoughtfulness, and treating both ourselves and others with respect are the hallmarks of a classy woman.

When I posted my video "8 Ways to Keep It Classy, Girlfriend!" I learned that the topic of classy behavior was really important to my listeners. The comments painted an amazing picture of what it means to act classy. Here is just a sampling of what my viewers wrote:

- **Take correction graciously**—no tantrums or passive-aggressive behavior.
- **Treat everyone with respect and kindness,** including those of lower social status, underlings at work, and those in the service industry.

- **Watch your alcohol intake** to avoid making a fool of yourself in public.
- **Do your best to be punctual and prompt**—don't disrespect others by keeping them waiting.
- **Listen with compassion and empathy** and look at people when they talk to you.
- **Don't leave mess and litter** in public places.
- **Don't think so highly of yourself that you make others feel inferior.** If someone makes you feel better about yourself, you probably just encountered a classy person.

Basic good manners is an essential part of this classy, respectful behavior. A classy woman always says please and thank you. She expresses gratitude humbly and with a smile on her face. If she bumps into someone or accidentally interrupts, she says, "Excuse me." And when she meets another person, she greets them pleasantly with a "Hi, how are you?" (instead of a grunted "Hey") and extends her hand. (Granted, during COVID days this preferred greeting turned into an elbow bump.) I know that some of these examples may seem perfunctory or even old-fashioned. But they truly make a difference in how we relate to one another.

When perusing social media, I'm often amazed at how many people these days seem to have lost (or never learned) how to behave politely and respectfully. Perhaps the biggest etiquette breach we all see today is the refusal to put down electronic devices at dinner or when someone enters a room. I'm amazed watching couples on a date; half the time they're on their phones. I know this is a cultural phenomenon and a generational one, but

I believe we must fight to teach our youngsters (and ourselves!) the value of device-free zones where eye contact and conversation are imperative.

I do want to mention the (almost) lost art of writing a thoughtfully worded note, especially a handwritten one. I think that means more in today's world than ever because it's such a rarity. A note expressing sincere thanks or sympathy is touching, thoughtful, and a wonderful example of class. It makes the recipient feel special. In the end, isn't that what being classy is all about?

Table Manners

Table manners is a particular subset of etiquette that seems to be going by the wayside. Scarfing down a hamburger with lettuce, tomato, and ketchup dripping down your face does not scream, *I'm a classy gal.* Eating slowly, taking smaller bites, and chewing with your mouth closed makes mealtime more enjoyable for everyone. So does a well-placed compliment to the person who prepared the food.

But class at the table doesn't just apply to how we eat but also what we choose to eat. A classy woman is one who is willing to expand her boundaries, including her palate. And when she tries something she doesn't care for, she responds with tact and grace. Saying something like, "I've tried it before and didn't love it, but I'm willing to give it another shot" is a wonderful response if served something you're not sure about.

It's all in how you convey and converse. Your openness to try and to explore new foods and new culinary experiences will make you a more well-rounded and cultured person. Who knows? Maybe you'll add something new to your repertoire.

The Power to Change It All

I believe we can make this world a classier place. I have seen firsthand that amazing things can happen when I make the effort to project myself well in the world—the doors that have opened, the opportunities that have arisen, the promotions I've received.

That's something worth considering if you feel like the wrong guy is showing up all the time, if doors seem to be closing when it comes to career opportunities, or if your social circle seems to have stagnated. Have you looked at the image you are projecting rather than only focusing on forces outside of yourself? Instead of blaming someone else or maybe assuming the role of victim, why not spend some time looking inward and asking yourself, *What am I doing to draw this in? Is there something I can change about me? Is there something new I can project?* I promise, it's an exercise that will pay off.

Ultimately, what you put out in this world is what you get back in return. Like it or not, we are judged first on the way we present ourselves. This is not a matter of people-pleasing or buckling under the judgments of others. It's just simple, commonsense acknowledgment of the way the world works. It makes sense to think about what your behavior and appearance say about you. What impression are you going to make so that more doors will open?

You have the power to change it all, so harness that power and do so with *class*!

NEXT STEPS

CHANGE ISN'T EASY.

If it was, then all people would be at their ideal body weight, in their dream job, married to Mr. Right, and feeling and looking their absolute best.

But change *is* possible. It's possible for *you*. And change like that is incredibly powerful.

When you choose to shine God's light on yourself, to look better on the outside and feel and do better on the inside, a force awakens.

When you choose to step out of your place of comfort and complacency and move toward the unknown in the name of self-development, that force is coming to life.

When you choose to abandon imagined fear and take bold steps of faith toward a calling, that force is on fire!

Every cell in your body is turned on. You feel it within—an internal communication about this new way of being. It's as if you're speaking a new language to yourself. And believe me: you are not the only one taking notice.

With this in mind, let me offer some words to prepare you for what may happen when the change in you starts to become obvious.

Life at the Crossroads

At first friends and family are often supportive and excited to see the changes within you. These might be the same people who were hoping you *would* change, encouraging you to do something different. But as we've seen, change can be scary, *especially* for those around you. You'll learn quickly who is in your corner, cheering you on for the long haul, and who isn't. Once you start to look *too* pretty, *too* lean, *too* smart, or *too* with it, suddenly they might start saying, "You're taking this too far" or "I don't know who you are anymore" or "I'm getting worried about you."

What's happening here? Your change might be awakening their own insecurities. The people around you might not be able to handle this new you, the one who is more confident, more assured, and a heck of a lot happier. Maybe, when they see you, they feel as though they are somehow falling short. Personal change can be like holding up a mirror to others, and if they're lacking in confidence or self-esteem, they might not like what they see. They may react by trying to bring you back down, simply so they can feel better about themselves without having to do any of the work you've been diligently putting in.

You've likely seen this kind of sabotage before. They'll hand you that pint of ice cream after you've sworn off dairy or discourage you from staying on your new path in any number of other ways. They'll say your change is inconvenient, time consuming, not fun. "What do you mean, you don't want to have pizza and soda anymore?"

This is an important crossroads for you, and some deep conversations with those around you might surface. And now is your time to speak your truth in a loving but direct way. Share what you're looking forward to, what new changes you want to make, what new discoveries you're anticipating. Encourage those you love to support these endeavors. You're looking to build your team, made up of people who are in your life to love, accept, and celebrate you. So you need to educate those around you about your new vision and the course you've set for yourself and let them know you're looking for cheerleaders, not saboteurs. You are not going back no matter what. So are they with you?

I've always believed that we are the company we keep. If those in your intimate circles are not serving you or vice versa, then it might be high time for some new company. This may sound harsh, and putting it into action can be painful, but you haven't come this far to be dragged back down to the depths of desperation and despair by naysayers and saboteurs.

Yes, you might need to part ways with some people who have been in your life for a long time. But you also have an incredible opportunity to surround yourself with new people who are on the same wavelength—a new team of positive role models, mentors, and encouragers. You can forge new relationships with like-minded individuals who will push you to do more rather than discourage you out of jealousy or their own desire not to evolve. If you want to climb higher, then choose to live life among achievers, doers, and go-getters. When you do, you'll be setting yourself up for the blessings to pour in.

Moving Forward Together

If you picked up this book, it's likely because you were searching for more. Maybe you believed there is something better but just weren't sure how to obtain it. Maybe you even doubted that you were worthy. At the very least, I hope you've moved beyond those feelings and have begun to feel some progress.

If you're on the younger side, then hopefully you see this book as an encouraging guide to living your best life and see me as your mentor, a role I joyfully choose. I hope my stories and advice have convinced you that the years ahead can be your absolute best. Yes, you will stumble and fall. That's an important part of life, and the learning is in the picking yourself up, dusting yourself off, and getting back on the road.

If your self-esteem is damaged due to abuse, neglect, poor decision-making, and a faulty belief system, I want you to know that changing the way you think and talk about yourself can take you from lacking to overflow. "You are your most valuable investment" should be a mission statement guiding your every move. Believe in yourself, love yourself, and make decisions that are based on what makes a better you.

Sharing my faith journey with you has been especially important to me. Your path might be similar to mine, and hopefully I've shown you that God meets you right where you are—that all you have to do is ask. Now I urge you to exercise your spiritual muscles and let God's Word show you that you are made in His image and that all things are possible. Let yourself feel worthy of His grace.

If you're a mature woman, I hope I've conveyed the power of the reset. It's never too late to rewrite your life's script. If you've reached a certain age, you've probably gone through some loss—loss of hormones, loss of perceived beauty, loss of sexuality, loss of a spouse, loss of purpose. But at any moment in your life, you have the ability to make a change in each and every area of your life—to look, feel, and be your best.

I believe we can be our own best friend as we age by not swimming against the current of what defines beauty in our society. Instead, we can start swimming parallel to shore. Let's be women who peacefully accept what can't be changed but who keep on doing what we can to be better.

Beauty has no age limit. Neither does happiness. It's my goal to embrace each passing year with open arms—with the courage to embrace what is, the will to change what isn't, and the faith to remain joyful through it all. I hope you will join me in that quest.

Writing this book is a prime example of my own life makeover. Its release comes just six months after I chose to end a twenty-eight-year news career and letting go of work that has been both lucrative and secure for me. And, as you've learned, there's been a shift in my personal life as well. Some major life decisions were being made, steeped in emotion, deep thought, counseling, and prayer. A giant shake-up that felt more like a simultaneous combustion. But sometimes, in the middle of machining through life, a small ping is heard. Ignored, it becomes louder—to the point where it's almost deafening.

I could have easily turned down the inner voice that called

me to write these pages. I had plenty of excuses: *I'm too busy. What if I don't have enough to say? What if I write it, but no one wants to read it? What will happen if I let go of a steady salary and choose to be my own boss? What if people respond badly to my authenticity?*

Well, what did I say about what-ifs?

Exactly!

Stepping Out on the Bridge

That brings me back full circle to my tagline: "Be bold and be blessed." If one woman grabs hold of my message and makes over her life in a way that brings her joy and meaning, then the years I've invested in this project will be well worth it.

I hope you know and feel how much I care about you. How I'm cheering you on—in my prayers, in this book, and in the content I produce on YouTube and social media. Your happiness and growth are the reasons I'm here. Your discovery of what makes you beautiful on the outside and radiant on the inside leaves me beaming with pride.

I am so honored that you've trusted me to guide you on this journey of self-discovery, the building of your bridge to a better you. It's being constructed by a woman who doesn't fear the hard work it takes to create it. A woman who is grateful for the struggle and the achievements and offers gratitude for each. A woman who knows when to hammer and drill and when to take a step back and exhale. A woman who realizes the bridge is not only for herself but for those she cares for and loves.

That bridge is a connector to her past and present, unlocking new appreciation and potential within.

It's a span for the passage of ideas, free movement, and discovery.

It's a foundation for a life to admire and love, stretching out as far as the eye can see.

You are that woman, and *this* is your bridge.

Godspeed.

ACKNOWLEDGMENTS

SPECIAL THANK-YOUS TO:

- Ioana and team at Kubis Interactive for your creative digital support.
- The vlogger in 2014 who said, "You need to start a YouTube channel!"
- The many viewers suggesting that I write a book.
- My pastors for pointing me in the right direction.
- Shannon Marven at Dupree Miller and my partners-in-prime at Nelson Books—a journalist's dream team!

NOTES

Chapter 1: Beauty from the Outside In

1. Bobbi Brown with Sara Bliss, *Pretty Powerful: Beauty Stories to Inspire Confidence: Start-to-Finish Makeup Techniques to Achieve Fabulous Looks* (San Francisco: Chronicle, 2012), 9.
2. Wikipedia, s.v. "expert," accessed June 4, 2021, https://en.wikipedia.org/wiki/expert.
3. Kevyn Aucoin, *Making Faces* (New York: Little, Brown, 1999).

Chapter 3: Bold and Blessed

1. Peter Freed, *Prime: Reflections on Time and Beauty* (New York: Peter Freed, 2015). For details about this self-published book and samples of the photographs, visit https://www.theprimebook.org. You can purchase the book directly from the site.

Chapter 4: The Unexpected Power of Rest

1. "1 in 3 Adults Don't Get Enough Sleep," Centers for Disease Control and Prevention, February 18, 2016, https://www.cdc.gov/media/releases/2016/p0215-enough-sleep.html.
2. Patti Neighmond, "Working Americans Are Getting Less Sleep, Especially Those Who Save Our Lives," NPR Shots: Health News from NPR, October 28, 2019, https://www.npr.org/sections/health-shots/2019/10/28/773622789

/working-americans-are-getting-less-sleep-especially-those
-who-save-our-lives.

3. Neighmond, "Working Americans."

4. https://www.nih.gov/news-events/nih-research-matters
/cool-temperature-alters-human-fat-metabolism.

5. Emily Cronkleton, "8 Natural Sleep Aids: What Works?"
Healthline, updated May 29, 2020, https://www.healthline.com
/health/healthy-sleep/natural-sleep-aids.

6. Gabrielle Kassel, "6 Chiropractor-Approved Exercises to Fight
Text Neck," Healthline, updated May 29, 2020, https://www
.healthline.com/health/fitness-exercise/text-neck-treatment#does
-text-neck-really-cause-pain.

Chapter 5: Fear, Faith, and Fuhgeddaboudit

1. Adrian Granzella Larssen, "7 Successful Women on the
'Mistakes' That Changed Their Careers," Fast Company,
September 20, 2019, https://www.fastcompany.com/90406108/7
-successful-women-on-the-mistakes-that-changed-their-careers.
Reshma Saujani's book is *Brave, Not Perfect: Fear Less, Fail More,
Live Bolder* (New York: Currency/Random House, 2019).

Chapter 7: The Magic of Mentoring (and Being Mentored)

1. "Become a Mentor," Mentoring.org, accessed May 5, 2021,
https://www.mentoring.org/take-action/become-a-mentor/.

Chapter 8: Keeping It Classy

1. "For Attractive Lips, Speak Words of Kindness," Quote
Investigator, July 8, 2013, https://quoteinvestigator
.com/2013/07/08/beauty-tips/. This quote was originally from
Sam Levenson, *In One Era and Out the Other* (New York: Pocket
Books, 1973), 177.

2. "Personal Quotes," Charlize Theron, IMDb.com, accessed May 4,

2021, https://www.imdb.com/name/nm0000234/bio?ref_=nm _dyk_qt_sm#quotes.

3. David Emer, "Angela's Assets," *Guardian,* September 29, 2001, https://www.theguardian.com/film/2001/sep/29/features.

4. Lexico US Dictionary, s.v. "grace," accessed May 4, 2021, https ://www.lexico.com/en/definition/grace.

ABOUT THE AUTHOR

EMMY AWARD-WINNING JOURNALIST Dominique Sachse has anchored the news for KPRC in Houston, Texas, for nearly twenty-eight years. Beginning her career as a traffic reporter and working her way up to the anchor desk, she quickly became a role model for women who sought her out for beauty advice and wisdom about life. In 2014 she launched her YouTube channel as a place to offer fashion, beauty, and lifestyle tips for women in their prime, and the response was enormous. Today she has nearly 2 million subscribers.

She balances her YouTube channel, content creation, and social media encouragement with her own practice of self-care, family commitments, and charity events.